ABSTRACTS *from* The STATE GAZETTE *of* NORTH CAROLINA

CRAVEN COUNTY NORTH CAROLINA

- 1796 -1799 -

(VOLUME #3)

Compiled by:
Raymond Parker Fouts

Southern Historical Press, Inc.
Greenville, South Carolina

This volume was reproduced
from a personal copy located in
the Publishers private library

Please direct all correspondence and book orders to:
SOUTHERN HISTORICAL PRESS, Inc.
PO Box 1267
Greenville, SC   29602-1267

Copyright 1982 by: Raymond Parker Fouts
Copyright Transferred 2023 to:
　　　　　　Southern Historical Press, Inc.
ISBN #978-1-63914-203-3
Printed in the United States of America

PREFACE

The data herein was abstracted from microfilm obtained from the North Carolina Department of Archives and History, Division of Archives and Manuscripts, Raleigh, North Carolina.

Advertisements are only recorded from the first issue in which they appear, though they may actually be in several subsequent issues. All issues located are included, though nothing was transcribed from them. Spelling and punctuation have been followed as closely as possible.

This work is indexed by the assigned number within parentheses preceeding each item. The calendars in the Appendix are included to give the researcher a quick reference to the date of "Sunday last" and the number of full weeks since the "18th ult.".

The originals of the following issues are retained by the listed libraries: American Antiquarian Society-10 May, 29 August, 31 October, and 26 December 1798; 2, 23, and 30 January, and 20 February 1799. Duke University Library-All issues of 1796; 5 January through 19 October 1797. Harvard University Library-2 November and 21 December 1797; 18 January, 1 February, 1 March, 24 and 31 May, 4 and 18 July, and 8 August 1798; 6 February 1799. All other issues are missing.

TABLE OF CONTENTS

Text   1-82

Appendix   83-86

Index   87-106

ABSTRACTS FROM THE STATE GAZETTE OF NORTH-CAROLINA

1796-1799

STATE GAZETTE OF NORTH-CAROLINA
EDENTON: Printed by Henry WILLS, Joint Printer to the State with A. HODGE.

Vol. XI. THURSDAY, January 7, 1796. Numb. 521.

(1) Territory South of Ohio, Knoxville, November 17. (Notification of taxes due for 1795 and 1796.) Willie BLOUNT. To the Proprietors of Lands in the Territory South of Ohio, resident in North Carolina.

(2) I hereby notify my creditors, and all whom it may concern, that I intend to take the benefit of the insolvent act, and come out of prison on the 10th day of January next. William WARBRITTON. December 24, 1795.

(3) Philadelphia, Dec. 17..Dec. 23. Arrived at Newburyport, schooner Nymph, Benjamin CLANNEL (?), master, 46 days from Larcahaye.

(4) Baltimore, Dec. 22. It is mentioned in a letter from Robert MONTGOMERY, Esq. Consul at Alicant, dated September 26, to a merchant at Marblehead...

(5) Petersburg, Dec. 29. It appearing, upon taking the enumeration of the inhabitants of the South Western Territory, that there are upwards of 60,000 free inhabitants therein, the Governor of said Territory..recommending to the people to elect five persons for each county..to represent them in a Convention, to meet at Knoxville on the 11th of January next, for the purpose of forming a Constitution, or permanent form of government.

(6) Norfolk, Dec. 31. Extract of a letter from York (Virginia) to a gentleman in this town, dated December 29. "On Sunday night last a full discovery was made of the robberies committed on the Mail. John GOOSELY, son of Capt. George GOOSELY, and John REYNOLDS, son of Mr. William REYNOLDS, both of this place, were discovered to be the perpetrators.. GOOSELY has made his escape, and an express has gone on to Philadelphia to apprehend REYNOLDS."

(7) Edenton, January 7. Married, _____ John HARVEY, Esq. of Perquimans, to Miss SKINNER, dau. of William SKINNER, Esq. Commissioner of Loans in this state.

(8) The subscriber having at the last county court of Chowan, administered upon the company estate of LOWTHER, HARDY, and LITTLE, deceased, requests all persons indebted to said estate to make

(8) (Cont.) immediate payment. John LITTLE. Edenton, Jan. 6, 1796.

(9) Dr. CUNNINGHAM, informs his friends, and former customers, that he has removed to the place lately occupied by Mr. B. GORDON, near the Folly, where all persons who may need his services will please to apply. Gates-County, Jan. 1, 1796.

(10) Thomas SEAMAN, Informs the public, that he carries on the Clock and Watch-Making Business, at his house, nearly opposite the Court-House, in Edenton,... Jan. 5, 1796.

(11) For Sale, At Windsor, on Saturday the 16th day of January next, The schooner Sukey, the property of Jasper CHARLTON, Esq... She is a Northern built vessel, of between 40 and 50 tons burthen... David STONE.

(12) North-Carolina, Pasquotank County, ss. Dec. Term, '95. The Jurors for the state and county aforesaid, do present that the county of Pasquotank is reduced to a situation of great peril and danger, in consequence of the proceedings of the society of people called Quakers-That the idea of emancipation amongst slaves is publicly held out to them... John LITTLE, foreman, James BOND, William JONES, Robert EGAN, Willis WILDER, James WOODWARD, William GOODWIN, Joshua WHITE, Charles LAUGHREA, Mason MIDER (?), Josiah HARDELL, J. P. FARTHAUTS, John BADHAM.

(13) State of North-Carolina, Pasquotank county, Dec. 17, 1795. Notice is hereby given..to all the creditors of Shubal COOK, of the town of Boston, in the state of Massachusetts..is dead, and that the subscriber qualified as administrator to his estate the last term of Pasquotank court... William BRUER, Adm.

(14) To Be Sold, On Friday the 8th day of January, at the dwelling-house of the late Charlton SIMONS, deceased, Sundry valuable Negroes ..also a good Riding Chair... John NORCOM, Adm. December 16, 1795.

(15) Dismal Swamp Canal. At a meeting of the President and Directors of the Dismal Swamp Canal Company, October __, 1795. Ordered, That the Shares, on which the payments heretofore required shall not be made on the 11th of January next..sold..at the Eagle Tavern, in the borough of Norfolk... Teste, Robert BROUGH, Clerk.

(16) Edenton. For Sale. A Tract of Land, lying in Northampton county, state of North-Carolina, containing 500 acres. This land is on Meherrin-river, and joins the town of Princeton (formerly called Pitch Landing). Another tract of 150 acres, about a quarter of a mile from the former, on Kerby's creek. Another tract, pine woods, 283 acres, lying about one mile from the latter. Also, a tract of 243 acres, lying in Southampton county, Virginia..terms made known by the subscriber, living in Princeton; Who desires that all persons having claims against him will make them known before the first day of January next, as he intends at that time to leave the state. Matt. FIGURES.

(17) Notice. Pursuant to an act of the General Assembly of this state, passed in the year 1715.. "That the Register of every precinct, when there is no Clerk of the church in that precinct, shall register all births, marriages and burials.."..the aforesaid act will be duly enforced by William BAINS, Register. Chowan county, Dec. 18, 1795.

(18) State of North-Carolina, Chowan county, December 24, 1795. Notice is hereby given..to all the creditors of Frederick NORCOM, senior, of the county aforesaid..is dead, and that the subscriber qualified as executor to his estate the last term... Richard BENBURY, Executor.

Vol. XI. THURSDAY, January 14, 1796. Numb. 522.

(19) Edenton, January 14. Copy of a letter from Demsey BURGES, Esq. Representative in Congress from this district...

(20) Died, on Friday night the 18th (sic) inst. in the 46th year of her age, after a long and lingering illness, which she bore with fortitude and resignation, Mrs. Sarah EGAN, consort of Mr. Robert EGAN, of this town. On Sunday evening her remains were respectfully interred in the church yard..a discourse, suited to the occasion, was delivered by the Rev. Charles PETTIGREW.

(21) Letters remaining in the Post Office, at Edenton, January 1, 1796. Obadiah BOSWORTH, Capt. Joseph BRYAN 2, Dr. Ryan T. BUTLER, Capt. John BULLOCK, Hezekiah BROADWELL, Mrs. BRIMAGE, Thomas CLARK, Susan COOPER, James CAMPBELL, James CHEW, John CAMERON, Hester CLARK, James DUNSCOMB, John DREW and Co., William ELLIS, John FRATER 4, Stephen FOWLER, Mrs. GOELET, William GLOVER, Dr. Chas. GRAHAM, John GOELET, Humphrey HARDY, Esq., HILL and PONS, Timothy HUNTER, Henry HARFORD, Major Richard HOWETT, Miles HARDY, John HILL, Walter HUBBELL, James B. JORDAN, Elizabeth JORDAN, H. I. KOCK, Joshua LONG, Benjamin LONG, Joseph LILLIBRIDGE, Esq., Azariah LONG, Mary MANDEVILLE, Malcom M'COLLOM, Abraham MASON, Malcom M'LELLAN, Esq., the executor or administrator of William M'COY, dec., Capt. Joseph MORRIS, Exum NEWBY, James NIEL, Mr. PRENTICE, David RICE, Miss Nancy SHERWOOD, Balow STURGES, John STRONG, Lemuel SUTTON, Joshua SKINNER, Chas. SPRUILL, John SMALL, Malachi WILSON, John WOOD, John WILLIS, Capt. Geo. WEST, John WYATT. Hend. STANDIN, A.P.M.

Vol. XI. THURSDAY, January 21, 1796. Numb. 523.

(22) Philadelphia, Jan. 4. Accounts from China, via Calcutta.. mention a very melancholy accident to..an excellent navigator, Capt. John KENRICK, of the American ship Lady Washington, while at the Sandwich islands. The Commander of another vessel..gave orders to salute the Lady Washington. His guns having been previously loaded with ball, which were..neglected to be drawn, one of the shot struck Captain KENRICK on the head, and killed at the same time an officer and two seamen.

(23) The Commissioners of the Sinking Fund, respectfully report to Congress, as follows:... Samuel MEREDITH, Esq. Treasurer of the

(23) (Cont.) United States.. On behalf of the Board, John ADAMS. December 18, 1795.

(24) Edenton, January 21. From a London paper of November 6, we understand, that the much celebrated Thomas PAINE is dead-that he died at the house of the American minister at Paris, of an abscess in his right side...

(25) Died, on Saturday last, sincerely regretted, William Johnston DAWSON, Esq. late a Representative in Congress from this district...

(26) Lately died, Mrs. Mary HARVEY, the amiable consort of Charles HARVEY, Esq. of Perquimans.

(27) The Subscribers have for Sale, between 250 and 300,000 18 inch Shingles, well seasoned, lying at one landing on Perquimans river, near Hartford. Any person wishing to purchase, will apply at their store, next door to Mr. H. STANDIN's, or to Capt. DUBOYCE, at Hartford. Elisha & Benjamin NORFLEET. Edenton, Jan. 19, 1796.

Vol. XI. THURSDAY, January 28, 1796. Numb. 524.

(28) Notice Is hereby given, to the heirs of Col. Spencer RIPLEY, (who are supposed to reside in the vicinity of Little-river, in Pasquotank county) that he lately died in Kingston, Massachusetts; and that the subscriber, of the same place, has administered on his estate; who requests that they may come forward and make application to him for their respective shares immediately. Seth DREW. January 16, 1796.

(29) To be Sold, at public vendue, on the premises, on Saturday, the 26th day of March next, as the property of the Trustees of the University of North-Carolina. A Piece or parcel of Land, lying in the county of Bertie, between the lands of Michael EVANS and James TURNER, beginning on Bachelor's Bay, and running back to Black-Walnut Swamp.. The above land is a part of the Duckenfield tract, and was left unsold by the Commissioners of Confiscated property. Alexander MILLEN, Attorney for Edenton district. Edenton, Jan. 23, 1796.

(30) To be Sold, remarkably cheap, A Good assortment of Woollen Cloths, Cutlery and Hard Ware,..just arrived from the manufactories in England..apply..to W. HUNTER, at Mr. EGAN's. Edenton, Jan. 26, 1796.

(31) Petersburg. Dec. 19. Between the hours of one and two o'clock on Sunday morning, a Fire broke out in this town, in the bake house of Mr. John DUGEON, in Old street, which soon communicated to 3 adjoining buildings, and burnt them to the ground...

(32) Edenton, January 28. Died, on Monday last; Dr. James HALSEY, of this town.

Vol. XI. THURSDAY, February 4, 1796. Numb. 525.

(33) Congress of the United States, House of Representatives, January 5. Robert RANDALL was brought to the bar attended by his two counsel; the Judge of the district of Pennsylvania likewise took his seat... RANDAL had, among other stories, told Mr. Samuel SMITH, that Mr. William SMITH should bring forward this land business in the house.. Mr. TILGHMAN..recapitulated the charges.. The first was an attempt to corrupt the men here. The second was his having said that thirty members of the House of Representatives had engaged to favour his scheme.

(34) To the Citizens of the State of North-Carolina. Whereas there have lately appeared in the State Gazette, presentments from the grand juries for several counties in the district of Edenton, wherein they present us, the people called Quakers.."as the authors of the common mischief in this quarter" which presentments...contain..sundry unjust reflections, absurdities and exaggerations... Given forth (in behalf of the society of people called Quakers) from our yearly meeting's standing committee, in Perquimans county, the 29th day of the 1st month, 1796. Signed by order and on behalf of the committee, Thomas JORDAN, Cl'k.

(35) Boston, Jan. 9. Shipwreck. On Wednesday night last, during the then violent snow storm, about 2 o'clock, the ship Margaret, Captain John MACKAY, from Amsterdam, for and belonging to this port, was cast away on the Gooseberry, near Baker's island, off Salem harbour, and the Captain, who was unwell, a Dutch gentleman passenger, one of the seamen, and the cabin-boy, were unfortunately drowned. Among the survivors is Mr. James LAMB, of this town, merchant, and part owner of the ship.

(36) Philadelphia, Jan. 9..January 14. Letter from Capt. David DEWAR, of the brig Eagle, dated at Nassau, New Providence, Dec. 25, 1795. "To Mr. George SIBBALD, Merchant in this ___, mentions that having sold the brig Eagle, at the Havannah, he took his passage in the Telegraph, Capt. MARRINER, and sailed from thence on the 11th do. for Philadelphia, that ___ days after they were cast away on the N. ___ end of the great Bahama Keys..after..seven days, they were taken off, by the Ranger privateer belonging to that place."

(37) Extract of a letter from Capt. Michael SMITH, to a gentleman in Newburyport, dated Algiers, September 9, 1795. "We are released from work-but must tarry here till we dispatch a vessel to Lisbon and return, by which conveyance I send this..."

(38) Extract of a letter from James SIMPSON, consul of the United States, at Gibraltar, dated..November 14, 1795,...to the Secretary of State...

(39) Edenton, February 4. Married, on Thursday last, Col. John HAMILTON, to the amiable Mrs. E. Sarah ENGS.

(40) State of North-Carolina. Tyrrell county, February 1, 1796. Notice is hereby given..to all the creditors of William MACKEY, of the county aforesaid..is dead, and that the subscriber has administered on his estate... Huldah MACKEY, Adm'x.

(41) New-York, December 31. Murder. A few days since a most horrid and inhuman act was committed by Matthias CUTLIP, at Newton, in the county of Sussex, on the body of his wife.. CUTLIP had been butchering some beef for a neighbour, and returned home something inebriated and says to his children, I have been butchering cattle today, and now I intend to butcher your mother! ..seized her and gave her three separate stabs, one of which was mortal!

(42) Dismal Swamp Canal. At a meeting of the Directors of the Dismal Swamp Canal Company, January 12, 1796. Ordered, that the holders of ____ pay to George KELLY, Esq. Treasurer, the further sum of Thirty Dollars on or before the first day of April ____ this being the seventh requisition... Robert BROUGH, Clk.

Vol. XI. THURSDAY, February 11, 1796. Numb. 526.

(43) Baltimore, January 23. Extract of a letter from Capt. Richard O'BRIEN, who has been in captivity in Algiers, above ten years, to a friend in Baltimore, dated Lisbon, 9th Nov. 1795. "I have the pleasure of informing you,..that on the 5th of September Joseph DONALDSON, Esq. agent of the United States, concluded a peace with the Dey and Regency of Algiers.. Mr. DONALDSON had it not in his power to redeem the captives immediately on obtaining the peace; but as soon as Col. HUMPHREYS arrives at Lisbon, he will facilitate their ransom..."

(44) Edenton, February 11. Monday last, was committed to the district gaol in this town, William BRIGGS, of Gates county, charged with the killing of William ELLIS, of the same county.

(45) The subscriber intends to leave the state some time in May next... H. NIELL. Edenton, February 6, 1796.

(46) New-York, Dec. 26. Deception. Extract of a letter from Newbern (N. C.) dated December 8, received by a respectable merchant in this city. "A false shipment appears to have been made in Philadelphia. A vessel arrived here a few days ago; the cargo consigned to Mr. Joseph TAGGART. The above was insured in New-York, as being on board the brig Betsey, Captain DOGGATE, who appears to be much deranged."

(47) Just Published, And for Sale, at the Printing-Office, (Price half a Dollar.) A Description of Occacock Inlet..Adorned with a Map, taken by actual survey, by Jonathan PRICE.

Vol. XI. THURSDAY, February 18, 1796. Numb. 527.

(48) By George WASHINGTON, President of the United States. A Proclamation.. I hereby give notice thereof; and that all cents and half cents, coined and to be coined at the mint of the United States from and after the said twenty-seventh day of December, are to weigh, the cents, each seven penny-weights, and the half cents, each three penny-weights, and twelve grains.. Done at the city of Philadelphia, on the 26th day of January, 1796. G. WASHINGTON. By the President, Timothy PICKERING, Secretary of State.

(49) Baltimore, February 6. Extract of a letter from Capt. William THOMPSON, of the schooner Brothers, of this place, to his friend in town, dated Grenada, Dec. 21. "..I was captured on the 18th instant, from Martinico bound to Trinidad, a Spanish port and neutral, by his Majesty's sloop of war, Favourite..."

(50) Edenton, February 18. Appointments. The President of the United States,..has appointed William CUSHING, Chief Justice of the United States; Samuel CHASE of Maryland, Associate Judge, vice BLAIR, resigned; and James M'HENRY, of Maryland, Secretary of War.

(51) The Subscriber intends to leave the state in a few days; he therefore desires all persons indebted to him to call and make payment in his absence, to Mr. Jonathan MALTBEE... Isaac MARQUAND. Edenton, Feb. 17, 1796.

(52) The Subscriber respectfully informs the public, that he will leave this place in ten days... Cyrus MARSH. February 18, 1796.

(53) For Sale, on long credit, Three or four hundred barrels of Indian Corn, lying in Musli-Island (?), on Roanoke river, seven miles above the town of Halifax. For terms, apply to the subscriber..or Mr. John RIEVES, in Northampton county. James BRADLEY. February 12, 1796.

Vol. XI. THURSDAY, February 25, 1796. Numb. 528.

(54) Hallowell, January 23. On the 5th inst. a very melancholy accident happened at Pittstown-As four boys of Mr. James DUNLAP were playing on the ice, three of them fell in; his daughter about 18 years of age, hastened to their assistance, and in endeavoring to relieve her three unfortunate brothers, perished with them. The parents were absent from home; two surviving small children left at home, crept into a bed, and remained there two days during the cold season, without sustenance.

(55) Worcester, January 27. Longevity. Mrs. Mary JONES, of Shrewsbury, relict of Col. JONES, late of Hopkinton, on Thursday last, compleated the 102d year of her age, on which day she rode a mile, to a friend's house, dined, spent the day, and took an active part in conversation with a number of other friends; one of which was Mrs. CUSHING, relict of the Rev. John CUSHING, late of Shrewsbury, in the 88th year of her age.

(56) Philadelphia, Feb. 8. Sunday last arrived in town James M'HENRY, Esq. Secretary at War.

(57) Edenton, February 25. Strayed or Stolen, On the night of the 17th instant, a dark bay Mare... George MORGAN. Edenton, Feb. 24, 1796.

(58) Gates County, February Term, 1796. The court order that this presentment be published in the State Gazette for one month. Law. BAKER, C. C. North Carolina, Gates County, ss. Feb. Term, 1796. The Jurors for the state and county aforesaid, present,

(58) (Cont.) that the country is reduced to a situation of great peril and danger, in consequence of the proceedings of the society of people called Quakers-That the idea of emancipation amongst slaves is publicly held out to them... K. BALLARD, Foreman, Thomas SMITH, Jonathan ROGERS, Demsey LANGSTON, William DOUGHTIE, Micajah RIDDICK, Rich. BARNES, Robert PARKER, Hillery WILBY, John PARKER, Mills LEWIS, James FREEMAN, Cypr. CROP, Moore CARTER.

Vol. XI. THURSDAY, March 3, 1796. Numb. 529.

(59) Feb. 19. Letter from Governor, New-York, January 19, 1796... John JAY (To) Robert Goodhue HARPER, Esq..

(60) Philadelphia, Feb. 10. A letter of the 8th December..from Lisbon, mentions that the brig Sophia,..Captain O'BRIEN, was to sail shortly after for Algiers, where she would take on board all the American captives, and sail directly for Philadelphia.

(61) Philadelphia, Feb. 11. Last evening arrived in town from New-York, Charles ADAMS, Esq..brought the Treaty..between the United States and the Dey of Algiers...

(62) Petersburg, Feb. 26. From Kentucky we learn, that the Legislature of that state have directed that application should be made to Congress to investigate a charge of perjury exhibited against Humphrey MARSHALL, one of the Senators of that state...

(63) Edenton, March 3. Old Harlequin, Will stand at Spring Hill, the plantation where the subscriber now lives, on the Head of Salmon Creek... John McGLAUHON, Bertie, February 24, 1796.

(64) Twenty Dollars Reward. Ran away from the subscriber, on the 14th ultimo, a negro man named PETER, about 5 feet 4 or 5 inches high, well set, of a very yellow complexion..about 40 years of age.. he is a shoemaker by trade.. Also a negro woman named JUDE, of a tall spare make, pretty black, about 30 years of age. They are both supposed to be lurking in this county, having relations at Mr. John BLOUNT's and Mrs. Mary BLOUNT's... William WHEDBEE. Perquimans, March 1, 1796.

Vol. XI. THURSDAY, March 10, 1796. Numb. 530.

(65) The Plan of Education to be observed and pursued by the Faculty of the University of North-Carolina, as adopted by the Board of Trustees the 4th day of December, 1795... Samuel ASHE, President.

(66) New-York, Feb. 13. Extract of a letter from James SIMPSON, Consul of the United States at Gibraltar, to Joseph M. YZNARDI, Consul General at Cadiz...

(67) Mr. FENNO, Be pleased to publish for the government of the merchants concerned, the following information communicated to me by the Secretary of State... Thomas FITZSIMONS, Chairman of the Committee of Merchants.

(68) Extract of a letter from Havanna, Jan. 23d, 1796, to a merchant in this city. "You will perhaps have heard..that the remains of Christopher COLUMBUS have been, by order of Court, transferred from the island and city of St. Domingo to this place, in a ship of 74 guns. The 19th instant they were deposited in the cathedral."

(69) Augusta, February 18. On Thursday last his Excellency the Governor made the following communication to the legislature... State House, Louisville, February 10, 1796... Jared IRWIN.

(70) Knoxville, January 19. On the 11th instant, the convention commenced their session in this town. The house proceeded to the choice of a president-his excellency William BLOUNT...

(71) Edenton, March 10. (University of North-Carolina) appointments were made: Rev. Samuel M'CORKLE, D. D. Professor of Moral and Political Philosophy and History. Rev. David KERR, Professor of Languages. Charles W. HARRIS, Esq. Professor of Mathematics. Mr. DELVAUX, Mr. HOLMES, Tutors in the Preparatory School.

Vol. XI.   THURSDAY, March 17, 1796.   Numb. 531.

(72) Edenton, March 17. The Printing-Office is removed to the third house east of the Court-House.

(73) Just landed, and for sale, by the subscribers, A Quantity of Figueira Salt..White Wine, in pipes, and Red ditto, in quarter-casks... Charles GRICE and Co.

(74) _____ Camden county, February 20, 1796. Notice is hereby given..to all the creditors of William WELROY, of the county aforesaid,..is dead, and that the subscriber has qualified as executor to his last will and testament February term last... Thomas ETHERIDGE, Ex'r.

(75) State of North-Carolina. Pasquotank county, March 10, 1796. Notice is hereby given..to all the creditors of Ambrose KNOX, of the county aforesaid..is dead, and that the subscribers qualified as executors to his estate the last term of Pasquotank court... John LANE, Hugh KNOX, Andrew KNOX, Ex'rs.

(76) State of North-Carolina. Chowan county, March 12, 1796. Notice is hereby given..to all the creditors of Jacob JORDAN, Esq. of the county aforesaid..is dead, and that the subscribers qualified as executrix and executor to his estate in September last... Elizabeth JORDAN, Ex'x., Nicholas STALLINGS, Ex'r.

(77) State of North-Carolina. Pasquotank county, March 10, 1796. Notice is hereby given..to all the creditors of Henry LANKESTER, of the county aforesaid..is dead, and that the subscribers qualified as executors to his estate, the last term of Pasquotank court... Robert M'MORINE, James L. SHANNONHOUSE, Ex's.

Vol. XI.   THURSDAY, March 24, 1796.   Numb. 532.

(78) Richmond, March 9. (Circular) Copy of a letter from John CLOPTON, Esquire, Representative of the people of this district, in the Congress of the United States, to his constituents. Philadelphia, February 22...

(79) Norfolk, March 14.. March 17. Extract of a letter from a member of Congress.."Judge CUSHING has..declined the acceptance of his appointment, as Chief Justice of the United States; this morning Oliver ELLSWORTH, of Connecticut, was nominated to the Senate by the President to fill the vacancy."

(80) Edenton, March 24. State of North Carolina. Hertford county, March 18, 1796. Notice is hereby given, to all the creditors of William Baker WYNNS, late of the said county,..is dead, and that the subscribers qualified as administrators to his estate last November term. Thomas WYNNS, Lawrence MOONEY, Adm'rs.

Vol. XI. THURSDAY, March 31, 1796. Numb. 533.

(81) ____ from Citizen ADET, Ambassador from the French republic, to the President of the United States... Faithfully translated from the original by Geo. TAYLOR, Jun., Chief Clerk in the Dep. of State.

(82) Extract of an address from Robert Goodlee HARPER, of South Carolina, to his constituents, containing his reasons for approving of the Treaty of Amity, Commerce and Navigation with Great Britain.

(83) Copy of an original letter, taken up at sea, enclosed in a bottle and handed us by Mr. George SINCLAIR, mate of the Schooner Eutaw, Captain STRAN, on his passage bound out. "Hogstye Keys, 15th August, 1795. This is to inform,..that on the 11th day of this month, we sailed from L'Anceveau, in the schooner Flying Fish, bound to Charleston. On the 13th, at 12 o'clock, we ran ashore here, and in one hour's time, the vessel bilged. We got our boat out, and the next morning got safe on shore. We made different trials to procure water, but in vain. One of our people named James TRACY, died through fatigue. We held a council, and concluded to proceed to Aukland's Key in our boat, with a small sail and two paddles. The names of the people are, Thomas BAILEY, master, James DUNSCOMB, mate, Benj. PARKER, merchant, Stephen LEVY, and Samuel MESTA, sailors."

(84) Savannah, (Georgia) March 3. In the House of Representatives, Friday, the 19th February, 1796. Whereas the most barefaced corruption has been practiced between some individuals of the companies who pretended to purchase under, and several Members of the late Legislature, which passed the usurped Act, "An act supplementary to an Act for appropriating a part of the unlocated Territory of this state for the payment of the late state troops..by which the western territory of this state was attempted to be bartered; and ..by the depositions on oath of Henry G. CALDWELL, James SIMMS, and Robert FLOURNOY, that..James GUNN (Senator) did attempt to corrupt and..influence some of the members of the said legislature which passed the law..." Extract from the minutes, James M. SIMMONS,

(84) (Cont.) Clk. H. R. In Senate-Read and concurred in. Will. ROBERTSON, Sec'y.

(85) Fredericksburg, March 18. On Thursday the 25th ult. at New London, Connecticut, departed this life suddenly, the Rt. Rev. Samuel SLABURY, D. D. Bishop of the protestant episcopal churches in the states of Connecticut and Rhode-island-and the first American Episcopate.

(86) Edenton, March 31. From Philadelphia, March 8. Yesterday the Supreme Court of the United States, now in session, proceeded to give their opinions solemnly in the case of WARE, administrator of JONES, &c. against HYLTON and Co. and EPPES.. it was a suit brought by the administrator of a British subject for a debt due from the defendants, who are citizens of the state of Virginia, before the revolution.. The cause was very ably argued..by Mess. Edward TILGHMAN, WILCOCKS, and LEWIS, for the plaintiffs, and Mess. MARSHALL and CAMPBELL for the defendants. The Court consisted of the Hon. William CUSHING, James WILSON, James IREDELL, William PATTERSON, and Samuel CHASE, Esquires, associate Judges.

(87) The Subscriber proposing to leave this state for a short time for the West-Indies, is under the necessity of requesting all those indebted to him to call and settle their accounts immediately. Claudius DAVID. Edenton, March 30, 1796.

(88) State of North-Carolina, Chowan County. To all Sheriffs and Constables..Whereas Thomas SATTERFIELD, Constable, hath this day made oath, before me, Samuel DICKINSON, one of the justices of the Peace for said county, that last night, having in custody a certain Cyrus MARSH, charged with having feloniously broken open a trunk, the property of John Peek CASE, and stolen therefrom gold to the amount of 200 dollars value, he..did make his escape.. Therefore in the name of the state, I charge and command you..to search diligently..and to make Hue and Cry after him... Edenton, the 28th day of March, 1796. S. DICKINSON (L. S.)

(89) Knoxville, Feb. 17. Copy of a letter from Silas DINSMOOR, Esq. agent to the Cherokee nation, to his Excellency Governor BLOUNT...

Vol. XI. THURSDAY, April 7, 1796. Numb. 534.

(90) Whereas the underwritten David HUMPHREYS, hath been duly appointed Commissioner Plenipotentiary, by letters patent under the signature of the President and seal of the United States of America ..30th March 1795, for negotiating and concluding a treaty of peace with the Dey and Governors of Algiers..he hath been further authorized to employ Joseph DONALDSON, junior...28th of November 1795. David HUMPHREYS.

(91) North-Carolina, Camden County, ss. Feb. Term, 1796. The Jurors for the state and county aforesaid, present, that the county is reduced to a situation of great peril and danger, in consequence of the proceedings of the society of people called Quakers...

(91) (Cont.) Cornelius GRAY, foreman, Ralph LEWIS, Willis SAWYER, Thomas BELL, Devotion SANDERLIN, Asa SAWYER, Noah GREGORY, Evan STANDLEY, Lemuel SAWYER, Myles JONES, Evan SAWYER, Stephen WILSON, John SPENCE. A true copy, Test, Malachi SAWYER, C. C. C.

(92) Sales by Auction. The subscriber has for sale, a general assortment of Goods, which will be sold..at his Vendue and Commission Store, on the parade, fronting the Court-House... Robert EGAN, V. M. Edenton, April 5, 1796.

(93) For Sale, By Robert MOODY, Ticklenburghs, London Porter in casks, Liverpool and Turk's-Island salt... Edenton, April 2, 1796.

(94) Fredericksburg, March 25. Early on Tuesday morning last, a Fire broke out in the town of Falmouth which consumed a valuable part of the town..the house occupied by Mr. USHER..and..the whole square, including the Tobacco Warehouse and the buildings of Mr. Gavin LAWSON, were wholly consumed...

Vol. XI. THURSDAY, April 14, 1796. Numb. 535.

(95) Philadelphia, March 27, 1796. (Letter from) S. SMITH (To) Mr. David STEWART...

(96) Edenton, April 14. The President of the United States has nominated to the Senate the following gentlemen, as Commissioners, being those contemplated in the treaty with Great Britain, viz. Henry KNOX, of Massachusetts, to settle the Eastern boundaries of the United States. Thomas FITZSIMONS, of Philadelphia, and James INNES, of Virginia, on the subject of British debts. Christopher GORE, of Massachusetts, and William PINCKNEY, of Maryland, of British spoilations.

(97) Notice. On Monday the 25th of this instant, will be sold, at the late dwelling house of John HUMPHRIES, Esq. deceased, part of his estate, consisting of Negroes, Horses, Cattle, Sheep... By the Executors. Currituck county, April 1, 1796.

(98) Twenty Dollars Reward. Ran away from the subscriber about the 15th of October last, a mulatto fellow named GEORGE, about 30 years old, of a low stature and well built, of affable speech and pleasant countenance. It is expected he may occasionally take a tour to Martin county, about Welch's Creek, to Captain Francis PUGH's in Bertie, where he has some relations, or to the head of Hoskey Swamp, in Hertford county, at all which places he has been heard of. Benjamin WILLIAMS. Cashie-Neck, April 7, 1796.

(99) A quantity of Tow Cloth. To be Sold, cheap, for cash, by PENFIELD & MARQUAND. Edenton, April 13, 1796.

(100) In the Philadelphia papers are published several letters which have passed between General GUNN, Senator from Georgia, and Mr. BALDWIN, a representative from the same state...General GUNN charges Mr. BALDWIN with having received papers from Georgia intended for public use, in which he was personally interested..

(100) (Cont.) General GUNN sent a challenge to Mr. BALDWIN, by Mr. FRELENGHUYSEN, a senator from New-Jersey..the same was a breach of the privileges of that House, on the part of James GUNN and Frederick FRELINGHUYSEN (sic)..having made apologies..no further proceedings were necessary.

Vol. XI. THURSDAY, April 21, 1796. Numb. 536.

(101) New-York. April 4. Last Thursday the ship Ocean, of Philadelphia, Captain VREDENBURG, 39 days from Havre-de-Grace..was taken possession of by the British frigate La Prevoyante, Captain BERESFORD, and sent for Halifax..several passengers..were permitted to jump into the long boat, and come up to town, among whom were Captain F. ARMOUR and young M____ NEXEN, son of Mr. E. NEXEN, merchant __ this city.

(102) Edenton, April 21. Caution to the Public. Extract of a letter from a gentleman in Philadelphia..received April 6, 1796. "A certain Elias Langford HERRING, a native of Virginia, has Committed a forgery on Col. HEASTER, of Reading, in this state, to the amount of 1470 dollars. A handsome reward is offered for him by the Governors of Pennsylvania, Maryland and Virginia. He is six feet high, has a blemish in one eye, black hair, dark complexion.. His father's name is William HERRING, is a tobacco planter, and lives near Dems River, Pittsylvania county, Virginia..."

(103) State of North-Carolina. Pasquotank county, April 14, 1796. Notice is hereby given, to all the creditors of Nathaniel PAINE, late of said county..is dead, and that the subscriber qualified as administrator to his estate in December term last... B. JONES, Adm.

Vol. XI. THURSDAY, April 28, 1796. Numb. 537.

(104) Letters remaining in the Post-Office at Edenton, April 1, 1796.- Isaac ARNETT, Benjamin ATKINSON, Reuben ARNOLD, Ellis Gray BLAKE, Mrs. Elizabeth BEASLEY, Obadiah BOSWORTH, Caleb BEMBRIDGE, James BOYCE, Lawrence BAKER, Lemuel BURKITT, William BROWN, Thomas COLLINS, Esq., John CAROLL, Henry COPELAND, Christopher DUCKITT, Col. W. R. DAVIE, Dr. Probard DICKSON, Capt. Abner DERBY, Monsieur DUPUY, 3, Christopher GAYLE, Thomas JORDAN, Joseph GARRETT, 2, Col. Tho's. HARVEY, Capt. Sylvanus HOWITT, Capt. Thomas JACKSON, Jonathan JACOCKS, William KITTER, Miss Nancy KERWOOD, Isaac LONG, William LEWIS, Richard LEMMON, John R. LANCASHIER, Duncan M'DONALD, Donald M'INNISH, Malcolm M'CLELLAN, Robert MARTIN, Mary C. MILLER, Edward MANING, Francis PERYNAUT, 6, Thomas POLLOK, Francis PUGH, George RYAN, Robert ROWAN, Martin ROSS, John ROBUCK, F. SPEREMENTS, William SCARBOROUGH, Benjamin SCARBOROUGH, Capt. Luther STEPHENSON, Robert SMITH, P. VOLFER (or VOLSER), John WALLACE, 2, Michael WILSON, Samuel WHITING, 3, Gurden WELLS, 2, John WOODARD. Lemuel STANDIN, P. M.

(105) Received, per the Experiment, Captain SMITH, a fresh supply of Summer Goods..at Hambleton WARRING's Store. Edenton, April 27, 1796.

(106) Whereas sundry persons in the adjacent counties have given in lands in the county of Perquimans..subject to pay a tax for.. 1795..unless they come forward immediately..part of them will be sold as will discharge the same. Edward HALL, Sheriff. Perquimans, April 19, 1796.

(107) Lost or Mislaid, On the evening of the 9th instant, A Note of Hand, from Matthew BRANTLEY, to me, for 12 pounds and two pence halfpenny currency, dated the 5th October, 1795..any person having found the same, will oblige me much by handing it to Mr. Myles O'MALLEY,...or to me by post. J. F. DICKINSON. Winton, April 18, 1796.

(108) State of North-Carolina. Bertie county, April 15, 1796. Notice is hereby given to all the creditors of Stevens GRAY, late of said county..is dead, and that the subscriber qualified as executor to his last will and testament at last February term... William Lee GRAY, Ex'r.

Vol. XI. THURSDAY, May 5, 1796. Numb. 538.

(109) Edenton, May 5. So far as the returns have been made..Sam. ADAMS, Esq. has a majority of votes as Governor of Massachusetts, and..will be re-elected...

Vol. XI. THURSDAY, May 12, 1796. Numb. 539.

(110) Newbern, April 19th, 1796. Pursuant to the notice of yesterday, the citizens of..Newbern assembled at the Court-house, to take into consideration, the propriety of presenting an address to the President of the United States, on the subject of his message in answer to the resolution of the House of Representatives on the 24th of March, 1796. Col. Joseph LEECH in the chair.. Ordered, That the foregoing resolutions be prepared for publication in Mr. MARTIN's Gazette of Saturday next...

(111) Mr. WILLS will be pleased to publish the inclosed letter from Demsey BURGES... Philadelphia, April 9th, 1796...

(112) New-York, April 21. Notice. The Citizens of New York, who are determined to support the constitution of the United States ..are Hereby earnestly requested Not To Attend the meeting to be held tomorrow in the fields at 12 o'clock... Wm. WILLCOCKS. April 21, 1796.

(113) The following is the letter..received by the committee appointed to enquire into the situation of the son of General LA FAYETTE: (Translation) "Rampagh, New Jersey, March 28, 1796..George Washington Mot___ LA FAYETTE. The Hon. Edward LIVINGSTON, Chairman, &c.

(114) Knoxville, April 1. On Monday last the first General Assembly elected under the constitution of the State of Tennessee, met in this town. Gen. James WINCHESTER of Sumner, is chosen Speaker of the Senate, and James STUART (?), Esq. of Jonesborough, Speaker

(114) (Cont.) of the House of Representatives..John SEIVER, the Governor Elect... April 13. On Saturday last, the General Assembly ..proceeded to the election of Judges of the Superior Courts of land (?) and equity, when John M'NAIRY, Archibald ROANE, and Willie BLOUNT, Esquires were elected. Landon CARTER, Esq. is elected Treasurer for the district of Washington and Hamilton, and William BLACK, Esq. Treasurer for the district of Mero.

(115) Died, at his house near Tellico blockhouse, on the 9th inst. SCODACUTTA, commonly called HANGING MAW, a great beloved chief of the Cherokees, aged about 65 years.

(116) Edenton, May 12. Saturday last, William BRIGGS, pursuant to his sentence at the late Superior Court, was executed on the commons, near this town, for the murder of William ELLIS, late of Gates County.

(117) Sales By Auction. On Saturday, the 21st inst. will be Sold, on Captain Samuel BUTLER's wharf...Salt..new butter..Chocolate, Coffee, Sugar... Robert EGAN, V. M.

(118) Notice. On the 2d day of June County Court next, will be Sold, on the premises, by public auction, The valuable Houses and Lots, belonging to Jasper CHARLTON, Esq. formerly occupied by William LOWTHER, Esq. deceased... Robert EGAN, V. M. Edenton, May 10, 1796.

Vol. XI. THURSDAY, May 19, 1796. Numb. 540.

(119) Copy of a letter from Mr. X. MICHAUX, (Botanist to the French Republic) to his Excellency Governor (William) BLOUNT. Fort Blount, on Cumberland river, March 2, 1796...

(120) Philadelphia, May 4. Appointment by Authority. Thomas NELSON, of Virginia, District Attorney, vice Alexander CAMPBELL, resigned.

(121) Middletown, April 29. Died; after a distressing illness of six days, George WYLLYS, Esq. Secretary of the State of Connecticut, in the 86 year of his age.

(122) Fayetteville (N. C.) April 28. We have the pleasure to inform..that General Thomas PEARSON, of Grenville county, hath lately presented the Trustees of the University of this state, with a donation of 500 pounds, for the use of that institution.

(123) Edenton, May 19. Married on Sunday last, Mr. Thomas HANKINS, to Mrs. Elizabeth WILLIAMS, widow of the late Mr. Willis WILLIAMS.

(124) Died, on Friday last, at Plymouth, Mr. William ARMISTEAD.

(125) Twenty Dollars Reward. Run away from the subscriber, on the 26th day of April, two French negro fellows, one by the name of ANTOMIS, a tall, likely, smooth faced fellow, about 21 years old..; the other, by the name of JOHN, a tall long favoured fellow..

(125) (Cont.) about 30 years old..deliver them to the subscriber, in Green-Ville, Pitt county... Oliver SMITH.

(126) Martinsburg, April 28. A most savage murder was committed last Sunday night, on the body of Mr. Nicholas YOUNG, an honest, aged citizen, living in the borders of Shepherd's Town.. No discovery has as yet been made of the perpetrators of this horrid deed.

(127) On the 2d of Feb. 1796, The Crew of the British Transport Aurora, Together with 9 German Officers, 130 Privates, 73 Women and Children, were saved when on the point of sinking, by the humane and generous exertions of Captain John HODGE, of the American ship Sedgely.

Vol. XI. THURSDAY, May 26, 1796. Numb. 541.

(128) Edenton, May 26. William BLOUNT and William COCKE (?), Esquires, have been chosen by the legislature of the State of Tennessee, to represent that state in the Senate of the United States.

(129) Married, on Tuesday last, Mr. William ROBERTS, to Miss Polly BENNETT, oldest daughter of Capt. William BENNETT.

(130) Whereas DREW & COPELAND, of Williamston, did, in October, 1794, give their bond to Messrs. James CAMOCK, & Co. for the sum of 900 pounds, Pennsylvania currency, payable in March, 1795; and whereas a receipt in full passed from the said James CAMOCK & Co. to the obligee; and the aforesaid bond may still remain in the hands of the said James CAMOCK & Co. This is to forwarn any person from taking an endorsement on said bond, as the same is fully paid and satisfied. William DREW, for DREW & COPELAND.

(131) Dismal Swamp Canal. At a meeting..May 21st, 1796. Ordered, That the shares on which the payments..not made on the 1st day of August next, be..sold to the highest bidder at the Eagle Tavern, in the Borough of Norfolk... Robert BROUGH, Clerk.

(132) Perquimans county, May Term, '96. This may certify, that it was..ordered, that this presentment be published for one month in the State Gazette. Test, John HARVEY, Clerk. The Jurors for the state and county aforesaid, present, that the county is reduced to a situation of great peril and danger, in consequence of the proceedings of the society of people called Quakers... T. BLOUNT, foreman, Nathaniel BRATTEN, Jesse TWINE, Abraham TWINE, Isaiah ROGGERSON, James REDDICK, Thomas STAFFORD, Lemuel FORBES, T. BATEMAN, Luke STALLINGS, Leaven THATCH, Lemuel BURKITT, Solomon RIDDICK, Joel HOLLOWELL.

Vol. XI. THURSDAY, June 2, 1796. Numb. 542.

(133) Norfolk, May 19..May 26. Rufus KING, Esq. is nominated by the President.., Minister Plenipotentiary of the United States, to the Court of London, and David HUMPHREYS, Esq. to the court of Madrid.

(134) Edenton, June 2. Married, on Tuesday evening last, Mr. James GRANBERY, of this town, to Miss Polly HARVEY, of Perquimans County.

(135) Notice. Offices of Inspection, will be opened in each county of the second survey, district of North-Carolina the whole of the month of June next, for the purpose of taking in entries of stills, elections, and granting licenses. H. MURFREE, Inspector of the second survey, of the district of North-Carolina, Murfreesborough, May 10, 1796.

(136) Advertisement. Will be Sold, on the 10th day of June next, pursuant to the last will and testament of Michael C. EVANS, deceased, That valuable tract of Land, lying on the sound, in Bertie county, known by the name of Scotch-Hall..whereon Mrs. LOCKHART formerly lived... The Executors.

(137) For Sale, Three or four hundred barrels of Indian Corn, on Roanoke river, five miles above Halifax town, Halifax county, state of North-Carolina... James BRADLEY. Mush-Island, Halifax county, May 8th, 1796.

Vol. XI. THURSDAY, June 9, 1796. Numb. 543.

(138) Tyrrell county, April Term, 1796. By the court it is ordered, That these presentments be published in WILLS's newspaper for one month. Test, S. CHESSON, Clerk. North-Carolina, Tyrrell county, ss. Jan. Term, 1796. The Jurors for the state and county aforesaid, present, that the country is reduced to a situation of great peril and danger in consequence of the proceedings of the society of people called Quakers... William STUBBS, foreman, Gideon COHOON, John HASSELL, William SPRUILL, Edmund HARRIS, Joseph ANSLEY, James HASSELL, Joseph ARNOLD, William BRICKHOUSE, George WYNNE, Philip HUNNINGS, Zebedee HASSELL. April Term, 1796. We the grand jury for the county of Tyrrell..recommend (this presentment) as highly deserving the strong arm of the legislature. Joseph PLEDGER, foreman, Edward WALKER, Jeremiah SEWAIN, James LONG, Russell ARMSTRONG, Willes DNOFER (?), Sackar WYATT, Thomas WILLIAMS, Samuel SPRUILL, Joseph HASSELL, James FRUNSON, Thomas EVERITT, Frederick DAVENPORT, John CLAYTON.

Vol. XI. THURSDAY, June 16, 1796. Numb. 544.

(139) Augusta, May 21. A Talk from James SEAGROVE, Esq. Superintendant of Indian Affairs, C. N. to the Kings, Chiefs, Headmen and Warriors of the Upper and Lower Creeks, Seminolas, and all other Tribes living in the Creek Land. Brothers,... Js. SEAGROVE, Superintendant Indian Affairs, C. N. (Copy) Attest. Zaca. LAMAR, S. E. D.

(140) Newbury-Port, May 26. Captain Charles GOODRICH, who arrived here on Thursday last, 24 days from Martinique...

(141) Dancing School. Harry Clay MILBURNE, respectfully informs the Ladies and Gentlemen of Nixonton, Hertford, Edenton, and its

(141) (Cont.) vicinities..at the Court-House in Nixonton, on Monday the 11th of July, in order to open a Dancing-School... June 13, 1796.

(142) Five Dollars Reward, Stolen or strayed, from the subscriber, about the 2d instant, a Sorrel Horse... William LAWRIE. Edenton, June 11, 1796.

(143) Hertford county, May Term, '96. By the court it is ordered That this presentment be published for one month in the State Gazette. Test, W. WYNNS, Clerk. North-Carolina, Hertford county, ss. May Term, 1796. The Jurors for the state and county aforesaid, present, that the country is reduced to a situation of great peril and danger, in consequence of the proceedings of the society of people called Quakers... Abner PERRY, foreman, Joseph BREDGER, Myles DAUGHTRY, Francis EVANS, William DOWNING, James NEWSOME, Thomas BROWNRIGG, James SOWELL, Samuel LUTEN, Elisha M'GLAUHN, Zabeech BRAMS, John YOUNG, George W. SESSUMS.

(144) (Top of page missing.) State of N. Carolina, Edenton District ss. April Term, '96. The Jurors for the state and district aforesaid, present, that the district is reduced to a situation of great peril and danger, in consequence of the idea of emancipation of slaves, held out by the society of people called Quakers, and others ... James HATHAWAY, sen., foreman, John NICHOLLS, Charlton WITHERINGTON, Timothy CARTWRIGHT, Benjamin COFFIELD, Lem. WILSON, Thomas POYNER, James Bruver JORDAN, Myles BENTON, John MULLEN, Frederick NORCOM, Thom. C. FEREBEE, John VAIL, William FAGAN, William STEPNEY, Jesse STALLINGE, Isaac BATWICK.

Vol. XI. THURSDAY, June 23, 1796. Numb. 545.

(145) A Charge delivered to the Grand Jury for the district of Virginia, in the Circuit Court of the United States..at the City of Richmond, May 23, 1796. By James IREDELL..Associate Justice of the Supreme Court of the United States.. Answer to the Honourable Judge IREDELL and Judge (C.) Griffin..By the majority of the Grand Jury, Henry LEE, Foreman. May 26, 1796.

(146) Salem, May 31. Extract of a letter from Capt. Asa BATCHELDER, of this port, dated Barbadoes, April 27...

(147) Edenton, June 23. Appointment by the President of the U. S., Frederick Jacob WICHELHAUSEN, Consul of the United States of America at the port of Bremen.

(148) State of North-Carolina. Chowan county, March 12, 1796. Notice is hereby given..to all the creditors of Calmetz DE LERTIER, late of Guadaloupe..is dead, and that the subscribers qualified as executors to his estate in March term last... Stephen CABARRUS, William BORRITZ, Ex'rs.

(149) State of North-Carolina. Chowan County, March 12, 1796. Notice is hereby given..to all the creditors of Jean Mathiese DE CALMETZ, son of Calmetz DE LERTIER, late of Guadaloupe..is dead,

(149) (Cont.) & that the subscribers qualified as administrators to his estate, in March term last... Stephen CABARRUS, William BORRITZ, Adm's.

Vol. XI. THURSDAY, June 30, 1796. Numb. 546.

(150) Jeremiah GALLOP, Has just received from New-York, an assortment of Dry Goods..to sell...

(151) Henry WILLS, Has just received from New-York, a small assortment of Dry Goods, Crockery, and Groceries, which he will sell..at the store formerly occupied by Michael PAYNE, Esq..

(152) Just Landed, Superfine fashionable coloured broad cloths, ... (fabrics, shoes, cutlery, etc.)... Charles GRICE, & Co. Elizabeth-Town, June 22, 1796.

(153) (Top of page missing.) Sold, at Plymouth, The brig Betsey, ..and the schooner Dolphin..property of Mr. William ARMISTEAD, deceased... The Executors. June 25, 1796.

(154) Notice. Will be Sold, at Public Vendue, on Friday, the 8th of July next, the late dwelling house of Mr. John B. SEGEAUD, deceased... The Executor.

(155) State of North-Carolina. Pasquotank county, June 8, 1796. Notice is hereby given..to all the creditors of Thomas MADREN, of the county afsd...is dead, and that the subscriber qualified as executor to his estate in June term last... John LANE, Ex'r.

Vol. XI. THURSDAY, July 7, 1796. Numb. 546. (sic)

(156) Philadelphia, June 10. Copy of a letter from Capt. James MOORE, of the ship Harmony, of this port, on the subject of a patent Machine invented by Benjamin WYNKOOP, for pumping foul air out of the holds of ships, by the motion of the ship at sea. Hamburg, April 5, 1796...

(157) New York, June 2_...June 21. Rufus KING, Esq. Ambassador to the British Court, sailed for London yesterday, in the James, Capt. COOKLIN, with his family.

(158) John Paul JONES. The directors of the Ohio company have advertised that the late J. P. JONES was proprietor of 5867 acres of land (?) purchased by the company of the North Western territory of the United States and desire his heir or heirs..to apply for the same at Marietta, in the said territory.

(159) Charleston, June 15. Again this city has been visited with the dreadful calamity of fire. Mr. Laurence CAMPBELL, Mr. Henry LANCHESTER, and Mr. Joseph VERREE, were considerably hurt while exerting themselves to blow up a house in broad street...

(160) Edenton, July 7. Simeon DE WITT, Esq. of the city of Albany, is appointed Surveyor General of the United States.

(161) State of North Carolina. In pursuance of the act of the General Assembly, entitled "An act to provide for the public safety by granting encouragement to certain manufactures; I issue this Proclamation, giving notice that Jacob BAYLOR, Sen'r of Buncomb county, in the district of Morgan..did, within three months after.. 1795, produce to me a sample of Rifle Gunpowder..part of..663 weight, made by him..and for which he claims the bounty.. At the same time, he produced to me a certificate under the hands of William TREADWAY, William BRITAIN, James ALEXANDER, Gabriel KIETH, and Edmund SAMS, Justices of the Peace for said county, and also under the hands of Henry WEST, Albert SMITHSON, Robert HARRIS, John WEBB, jun'r. and John JOUSH (?), freeholders of said county, certifying that they had seen the said Jacob..make different parcels of the Rifle Gunpowder.. Given under my hand this 10th of April, 1796. Samuel ASHE.

(162) John VAIL, Has just received from New-York, an assortment of Spring Goods, Crockery and Groceries...

(163) For Sale, That well known Tract of Land, whereon the subscriber now lives, in the county of Perquimans, containing 400 acres, about 3 miles from the town of Hertford, on the main road from that to Edenton; whereon is a very good dwelling house, kitchen, smoke-house, barn, stables, &c... William CLEMONS. Perquimans county, July 4, 1796.

(164) Notice. The Subscriber informs the public, that he has.. Summer Goods..also all kinds of Wet Goods..Port, Sherry and Teneriffe Wine, Rum, Molasses, Coffee, Sugar, Chocolate, Starch, Soap, Candles, Allspice, and Pepper. Claudius DAVID.

Vol. XI. THURSDAY, July 14, 1796. Numb. 547.

(165) State of North-Carolina. Chowan county, July 8, 1796. Notice is hereby given..to all the creditors of Robert HARDY, of the county aforesaid..is dead, and that the subscriber qualified as administrator to his estate, in June term last... Frederick RAMCKE, Adm'r.

(166) Philadelphia, June 24...July 1. On Friday last arrived at Carlisle, Major General Anthony WAYNE...

(167) Edenton, July 14. Died, on Tuesday morning last, Miss Nancy EARLE, of this county.

(168) Letters remaining in the Post-Office, at Edenton, July 1, 1796. Daniel BRUCE, Mrs. BRIMAGE, William BENT, Joseph BLOUNT, Mrs. Susannah CHARLES, Jasper CHARLTON, John COWPER, Capt. Thomas COOK, Monsieur DUBOIS, Stephen DIROLL, Henry FLURY, James FRASIR, John GLOVER, William HUNTER, George HAM, Anson HUBBELL, HILL and PONS, Josiah HUSLRY (?), Jas. HUMPHREY, James B. JORDAN, John JOHNSON, Mrs. IMIS (?), Mrs. Elizabeth JORDAN, King LUTON, Lemuel SUTTON, Mrs. Rebeccah LONG, Thomas LONG, Capt. William MARSHALL, Saros MARTH, Jeremiah MIXON, Edward MANNING, Robert MARTIN, John NICOLLS, Francis PUGH, John ROEBUCK, Gilbert RODMAN, Hezekiah STONE, Esq., David STONE, Esq., Evan SIMPSON, Mrs. Martha THORN, Capt. Henry D.

(168) (Cont.) THOMPSON, John WILLIS, Esq., John WOODWARD, Rev. Lewis WHITFIELD, Mr. WHITE, Miss Betsey WEST, Hend. STANDIN, A. P. M.

(169) Ran Away from the subscriber, on the 27th inst. an apprentice boy by the name of John TURNER, alias POOL, about 18 years of age, of a light complexion, and long brown hair... Thomas JORDAN. Pasquotank county, 29th of 6th month, 1796.

(170) Philadelphia, June 23. By the schooner Renwick, Capt. HUNT, 17 days from Barbadoes, we have received the following..from Capt. Wyatt ST. BARBE, of the ship Enterprize, belonging to Wiscasset.

Vol. XI. THURSDAY, July 21, 1796. Numb. 548.

(171) Edenton, July 21. John STEELE, Esq. of this state, is appointed Comptroller of the Treasury, vice John DAVIS of Massachusetts resigned.

(172) The subscriber wishes to hire by the week, a Negro Wench, who understands cooking, washing, ironing, and waiting in the house, ..apply at the house formerly occupied by Mrs. BARKER, deceased. Martin SHEEL. Edenton, July 19, 1796.

(173) The subscriber has for sale, a quantity of Peruvian Bark.. very lately imported from Cadiz..to accomodate families that may be in want of that most useful and necessary medicine. William LITTLEJOHN. Edenton, July 19, 1796.

Vol. XI. THURSDAY, July 28, 1796. Numb. 549.

(174) Albany, July 1. We are informed a treaty is now holding at Buffaloe Creek between the proprietors of the Connecticut Western Reserve, and certain tribes of the Indians. General CLEVELAND is at the treaty, and the Hon. Mr. Oliver PHELPS on his way thither.

(175) To the Citizens of the district of Edenton. Gentlemen, I again offer myself a candidate to represent the District of Edenton in Congress... Demsey BURGES.

(176) Dancing School. The subscriber wishes to inform..that he has left his subscription list with Mr. Myles O'MALLEY..and that he will attend on Monday, the 19th of September next, at Mrs. RONDET's..in order to open a school. Harry Clay MILBURN.

(177) For Sale, A Tract of Land, in Perquimans county, containing 300 acres, about two miles from the town of Hertford, near the main road..to Edenton..a good new dwelling house, kitchen..apple orchard..peach orchard and nursery... Thomas CREECY. Perquimans, July 25, 1796.

Vol. XI. THURSDAY, August 5, 1796. Numb. 550.

(178) Fayetteville, July 16. At a..meeting of the inhabitants of

(178) (Cont.) the county of Cumberland and town of Fayetteville.. on Wednesday, July 24 (sic), 1796, for the purpose of expressing their opinion on the late measures of Congress: George ELLIOT, Esq., Chairman, and Joshua WINSLOW, Esq. clerk. Resolved unanimously, That the conduct of Wm. B. GROVE, Esq. during the late session of Congress, meets our warmest approbation... Geo. ELLIOT, Chairman. Joshua WINSLOW, Clerk. Answer... William Barry GROVE.

(179) Springfield (Mass.) July 5. Mr. Jabez HERDRICK, of South Wilbraham, (Mass.) has formed a model of a machine to calculate Longitude with the greatest exactness. Also a dial to tell the time of night by stars...

(180) New London, July 16. Capt. P. BENJAMIN, of the brig Nancy, of Norwich, had his vessel and cargo condemned at Grenada, on the 2d June last, as American property...

(181) New-York, July 15. On Friday, July 1_ died, Abraham YATES, jun. Mayor of the city of Albany.

(182) Edenton, August 6. Those persons having demands on the estate of William F. DAWSON, late of Bertie county, deceased, are requested to inform Samuel TREDWELL, Esq.... P. DAWSON, Adm'x. July 27, 1796.

(183) Albert GALLATIN, who is well known in Congress, was a citizen of Geneva, of a very respectable family. Upon his arrival (in America) he was highly recommended..to..Dr. COOPER of Boston, who introduced him as an instructor in the French language in the University of Cambridge.

Vol. XI. THURSDAY, August 11, 1796. Numb. 551.

(184) Edenton, August 11. The partnership of the Subscribers, under the Firms of Watson STOTT, and Co. at Suffolk, Ebenezer STOTT, and Co. at Petersburg, Virginia; and Robert DONALDSON, and Co. at Fayetteville, North-Carolina, terminated on the 31st ultimo. Messrs. J. HATTERSLEY, and William FISHER, are authorised, in the absence of Watson STOTT, to collect the debts and settle the business of the store at Suffolk.... Watson STOTT, Ebenezer STOTT, Robert DONALDSON, August 1st, 1796.

(185) United States of America, North-Carolina District. These may certify..that Capt. Joseph BOZMAN, hath this day paid up the judgement obtained by the United States against him, and that he accordingly is released from his prison bounds. Michael PAYNE, Marshal, North-Carolina District. Edenton, August 9, 1796.

(186) Having settled the accounts of the estate of Edmund BLOUNT, Esq. deceased, which were committed to my care... James SUTTON. Edenton, August 5th, 1796.

(187) State of North-Carolina. Tyrrell county, August 8, 1796. Notice is hereby given..to all the creditors of Thomas LEE, of the county aforesaid..is dead, and that the subscriber qualified as

(187) (Cont.) executor to his estate in July term last... Edmund BLOUNT, Ex'r.

Vol. XI. THURSDAY, August 18, 1796. Numb. 552.

(188) Philadelphia, August 4. The Western Posts taken possession of. Extract of a letter from Capt. James BRUSS (or BRUFF), to the Secretary of War, dated Fort Oswego on Ontario, July 15, 1796...

(189) Edenton, August 18. At the late election, the following gentlemen were chosen to represent the county of Chowan and town of Edenton in the General Assembly. Lemuel CREECY, senate. Richard BENBURY and Benjamin COFFIELD, commons. Thomas JOHNSON, for the town.

(190) Ten Dollars Reward. Run Away from the subscriber, on Friday, the 12th inst. a likely young negro fellow by the name of HARRY, he is of a dark complection and well made, about 5 feet 7 or 8 inches high... Nathaniel HOWCOTT.

(191) Supervisor's Office, July 15, 1796. Officers of Inspection will attend in each county of the state of North-Carolina, during the month of September, to receive Entries of Carriages, and grant certificates to owners... William POLK, Supervisor of the Revenue District of North-Carolina.

(192) On Saturday, the 24th of September next, will be Sold, The valuable houses and lots in the town of Hertford, now occupied by Mrs. DONALDSON, together with the ferry..to the highest bidder, for ready money, to satisfy an execution, at the instance of Charles MOORE's executor against Andrew DONALDSON's administratrix... Edw. HALL, Sheriff. August 1_, 1796.

(193) State of North-Carolina. Currituck county, June 4, 1796. Notice is hereby given, to all the creditors of John HUMPHRIES, Esq., late of said county..is dead, and that the subscribers qualified as executors to his last will and testament at last May term... Joseph FEREBEE, Samuel FEREBEE, Ex'rs.

Vol. XI. THURSDAY, August 25, 1796. Numb. 553.

(194) Edenton, August 25. Demsey BURGES, Esq. is re-elected a member of the House of Representatives of the United States for this district. Nathan BRYAN, Esq. we understand, has been re-elected a Representative in Congress for the district of Newbern.

(195) Members of the Assembly chosen at the late Election. Perquimans-Joseph HARVEY, senate. Charles HARVEY and William BLOUNT, commons. Pasquotank-John HAMILTON, senate. John LANE and Baily JACKSON, commons. Camden-Nathan SNOWDEN, senate. Enoch DAILY and Joseph MORGAN, commons. Currituck-Joseph FEREBEE, senate. Thomas WILLIAMS and Jesse SIMMONS, commons. Tyrrell-Richard HOWETT, senate. John GUITHER and Charles SPRUILL, commons. Gates-Joseph RIDDICK, senate. James GATLING and John B. WALTON, commons. Bertie-Timothy WALTON, senate. John JOHNSON and George OUTLAW, commons. Hertford-

(195) (Cont.) Thomas WYNNS, senate. Robert MONTGOMERY and Henry HILL, commons. Martin-Ebenezer SLADE, senate. John STEWART and John HYMAN, commons. Halifax-S. W. CARNEY, senate. J. A. TABB and Eaton PUGH, commons. Town of Halifax-William R. DAVIE. Northampton-John M. BINFORD, senate. Benjamin WILLIAMSON and Henry PETERSON, commons. Edgcomb-Nathan MAYO, senate. John LEIGH and Bethell BELL, commons.

(196) Taken up and committed to the gaol of this town, about the 1st instant, a negro wench by the name of PRUDENCE, of about 60 years of age, who says she belongs to Nicholas LEWIS near Halifax... Charles ROBERTS, Sheriff. Edenton, August 24, 1796.

Vol. XI. THURSDAY, September 1, 1796. Numb. 554.

(197) Salem, August 9. Captain John BARTON, from Rochfort, informs that the celebrated Captain BARNEY, late of Baltimore, has the command of a squadron of frigates, eight in number.

(198) Edenton, September 1. Thomas BLOUNT, Esq. has been re-elected to represent the Halifax Division of this state in the Congress of the United States, by a large majority. William Barry GROVE, Esq. has also been re-elected by a large majority as Representative in Congress for the Fayetteville Division.

(199) State of North-Carolina. Pasquotank county, August 30, 1796. Notice is hereby given..to all the creditors of Hezekiah WOODLEY (?), of the county aforesaid..is dead, and that the subscriber qualified as administrator to his estate in June term last... Reuben KEATON, Adm'r.

(200) State of North-Carolina. Pasquotank county, August 30, 1796. Notice is hereby given..to all the creditors of Joshua POOL, of the county aforesaid..is dead, and that the subscriber qualified as administrator to his estate in June term last... Reuben KEATON, Adm'r.

Vol. XI. THURSDAY, September 8, 1796. Numb. 555.

(201) Edenton, September 8. We hear that General Charles Cotesworth PINCKNEY, of South-Carolina, is to succeed Mr. MONROE, as minister Plenipotentiary of the United States to the French Republic.

(202) Taken by execution, and to be sold..the 24th day of October next..a valuable piece of Land, situate in Gates County, about six miles from Col. William BAKERs store, and one mile from Mr. GONDYs near the Virginia road, leading from Mr. BAKERs, containing about 700 acres, on which is a dwelling, and other out houses, to satisfy a judgement obtained by Samuel DONALDSON, surviving partner, against Isaac WATERS. Michael PAYNE, Marshal, North-Carolina District. Edenton, Sept. 6, 1796.

(203) Grang (sic) Lodge. The Officers and Members of the Grand Lodge,..are hereby requested to attend the Annual Communication at the Lodge Room, in the city of Raleigh, on the 24th (?) day of November next. By order of the most Worshipful W. R. DAVIE, G. Mas-

(203) (Cont.) ter. Robert WILLIAMS, Jun., G. Secretary. August 29.

(204) For Sale. A Valuable Survey of Land, located the 14th (?) day of March, 17_4, under the particular direction of Col. Hardy MURFREE, containing 3,840 acres, granted to the subscriber for military services, lying in the county of Davidson, near Nashville, in the South Western Territory, State of Tennessee; the patent and plot may be seen..by applying to Mr. Alexander MILLEN, or the subscriber, at Edenton... Clement HALL. Edenton, September 2d, 1796.

Vol. XI. THURSDAY, September 15, 1796. Numb. 556.

(205) New-York, August 24. Extract of a letter from Capt. James NEIL of the brig Mary Ann, dated Cadiz, July 22, 1796...

(206) Newbern, August 27. Extract from the Log-Book of Capt. Alex. DUGUID, who arrived here on Thursday last from St. Thomas's...

(207) Edenton, September 15. Copy of a letter from Capt. SMITH, of the ship Harmony, to his owner in Philadelphia... Robert SMITH.

(208) State of North-Carolina. Pasquotank county, September 14, 1796. Notice is hereby given..to all the creditors of Lemuel PALIN, of the county aforesaid..is dead, and that the subscribers qualified as administrators to his estate in last Pasquotank court... Andrew KNOX, Hugh KNOX, Adm's.

(209) North-Carolina, Comptroller's Office, August 24. The Clerks of courts within this state, who have failed to furnish the..returns required by law to this office, will be subject to the expence of having them sent for... J. CRAVEN, Comptroller.

(210) Boston, August 16. On Friday last sailed from this harbour the sloop Portland Packet, THURLO, in government service, bound for Halifax, having on board the Hon. David HOWELL, Esq. Commissioner on the part of the United States, to determine our Eastern boundary, the Hon. James SULLIVAN, Esq. agent in the same business; and several gentlemen passengers...

Vol. XI. THURSDAY, September 22, 1796. Numb. 557.

(211) Edenton, September 22. We hear from Halifax that the Hon. Joseph M'DOWELL, of Morgan, and Nathaniel MACON, of Warrenton, are elected Representatives in the ensuing Congress, for their respective districts.

(212) Lottery. Whereas..the opening of a small creek (called Little Flatty Creek) and the cutting a Canal therefrom, not exceeding two miles, up into our neighborhood, in the lower part of the county of Pasquotank, and state of North-Carolina..would tend greatly to the convenience of the inhabitants..we have adopted the following Scheme of a Lottery.. The drawing will be in the town of Nixonton, under the direction and inspection of Thomas HARVEY, John SHAW, Rowan HOWETT, William T. MUSE, and Frederick B. SAWYER, Esquires... Thaddeus FRESHWATER. Reuben KEATON. Scheme of Bridgfield Canal Lottery.

(213) The 31st of July, I sent a letter containing a note of the United States Bank in Philadelphia, No. 79 value, for 100 dollars.. to Mr. August KONIG, merchant in Baltimore, after this I sent 3 letters to Mr. August KONIG, and to this day not received any answer, I request the favour of Mr. KONIG to let me know in the newspapers, if my first letter with 100 dollars, and the 3 other letters are come to his hands. Martin SHEEL. Edenton, Sept. 21st, 1796.

Vol. XI. THURSDAY, September 29, 1796. Numb. 558.

(214) Philadelphia, Sept. 12. Extract of a letter from a merchant in Statford (Connecticut) to his friend in New-York, dated the 9th instant. ..About 10 o'clock at night, the store belonging to Mr. Isaac TOMLINSON,..was discovered to be on fire; the neighbors were called and put it out...

(215) September 13. It is important that the citizens of the United States should be early apprised of the President's intention to decline standing a candidate at the next election. It requires no talent at divination to decide who will be candidates for the chair. Thomas JEFFERSON and John ADAMS, will be the men...

Vol. XI. THURSDAY, October 6, 1796. Numb. 559.

(216) State of North-Carolina. Chowan County, October 3, 1796. Notice is hereby given..to all the creditors of Ann EARL, deceased, that the subscriber qualified as an executor, in September term last... Jacob BLOUNT, Ex'r.

(217) Agreeable to the last will and testament of Ann EARL, dec. will be Sold, at public vendue, at Mrs. Elizabeth JOURDANS, 15 miles above Edenton, on Thursday, the 27th day of this instant, 25 likely Negroes..Corn, Peas, Brandy and several other articles... The Executor. October 3d, 1796.

(218) Fifteen Dollars Reward. Run away from the subscriber, a Negro Fellow, about 20 years of age, by the name of ABRAM..he has two of his upper fore teeth out, by reason of a stroke in fighting, very large feet, hands and wrist, about 5 feet 8 or 9 inches high; I suppose he has endeavoured for Edenton, as that noted villain Mr. EAGAN's DUN, is his father..bring him to me at Woodstock, Hyde county... William DAILY. August 25, 1796.

(219) Three Hundred Dollars Reward. Stolen from the subscriber, on the 28th ult. a red Morocco pocket book, containing 1500 dollars, in Philadelphia Bank Notes, and a great many letters in the French, Danish, English and German languages, and a certificate from the Free-Masons in Baltimore, also a small trunk..containing one gold watch..two gold seals,..another lady's watch with a gold chain, and gold hook,..a pair of pearl ear rings, with a small diamond, one gold necklace..a green silk purse, marked M. S. containing 200 Dutch ducats and 20 guineas, 12 fine ruffled shirts, marked S. 48, two dozen pair of silk stockings, marked S. Martin SHEEL. Edenton, October 4, 1796.

(220) State of North-Carolina. Chowan County, October 3, 1796. Notice is hereby given, to all the creditors of Jacob SIMONS, of the said county..is dead, and that the subscriber qualified as administrator, on the estate of the said deceased, in last September term... John SIMONS.

(221) State of North-Carolina. Chowan County, October 3, 1796. Notice is hereby given, to all the creditors of George BAINS, jun., of the said county..is dead, and that the subscriber qualified as administrator, on the estate of said deceased, in last September term... Lemuel CREECY.

(222) List of Letters remaining in the Post-Office at Edenton, October 1, 1796. Joseph A. BROWN, Joseph BENNET, Citoyen BERRENGER, Alexander BLACK, John BANBURY, William CRAWFORD, Mary CAREY, Capt. Samuel CABB, Thomas CLARKE, John COWPER, Gates county, James CRAWFORD, Iredell county, Caleb ELLIOT, Jonathan GOODWIN, Josiah GRANBERY, John GOELET, Capt. John GUYTHER, John HARWOOD, 3, John HENDERSON, Charles HUNT, Walter HUBBELL, Archibald JETT, Wake county, Benoice JOHNSON, William KITTER, Tristram LOWTHER, Joseph LISTE, Richard LEMMON, Edw'd. MANNING, John MANN, Capt. William MALEY, Axum NEWBY, Alexander OLIVER, Scuppernong, Timothy OSGOOD, Stephen OUTERBRIDGE, Francis PEYRENNAUT, 5, Patrick RELLY, Robert ROWAN, Goston RONOK, Isaac SEABOURN, Abner STUBBS, Capt. Samuel STODDARD, Evan SKINNER, Tyrrell county, F. SPEREMENTS, James SAUNDERS, schoolmaster, Abel ASHLY, John WARRING, Capt. John WILLIAMS, of brig Betsey, Elizabeth WILLIAMS, Michael WILSON, John WOODWARD, Mess. WEBB, BRYER and Co., John YOUNG, Gurden WELLS. Lemuel STANDIN, P. M.

Vol. XI. THURSDAY, October 13, 1796. Numb. 560.

(223) Norfolk, October 2 (?). Extract of a letter from Robert and John MONTGOMERY (?), dated Alicant August 6th, to F.____ and Son, at Lisbon. "We have received a letter from the American Consul at Marseilles, dated 22d June, advising that a Dutch ship had arrived at the place of Quarantine from Algiers, with all the Americans on board, who had been prisoners at that place."

(224) Denton (sic) (Edenton), October 13. The following account of James HULL, who was ten years a prisoner in Algiers, is taken from a Charleston paper: "James HULL was born in Smithfield, and was brought up in Petersburg, Virginia-he is about 30 years old and left the said place about 12 years ago. After having been at South Quay, Charleston and Baltimore, he shipped on board a brig commanded by Captain COFFIN, bound to Teneriffe, and from thence to Dunkirk; he there took his passage to St. Ubes, on board an American ship commanded by Capt. O'BRIEN; two days after they left St. Ubes, on their passage to America, they were captured by an Algerine corsair, and were taken into Algiers, where the said James HULL remained a slave ten years..HULL, about 12 months ago,...(was) shipped on board one of those vessels that sailed to the coast of Scilly..she was taken by a Neapolitan frigate, who carried her to Palermo. The Algerines were made slaves and HULL was released.

(225) Dismal Swamp Canal. At a Meeting of the President and Direc-

(225) (Cont.) tors of the Dismal Swamp Canal Company, Sept. 7, 1796. Pursuant to a resolve of the last General meeting of the Company: It is Ordered, That books be opened according to law for an additional subscription of Eighty Shares in the Canal, on the first day of November next, in Virginia, under the management of Robert ANDREWS, Esq. in Williamsburg, of Alexander MACAULEY, Esq. in York, of George KELLY, Esq. in Norfolk, of Richard BLOW, Esq. in Portsmouth, of Thomas SWEPSON, Esq. in Suffolk, of William DOUGLAS, Esq. in Petersburg, of James M'CLURG, Esq. in Richmond, of Benjamin DAY, Esq. in Fredericksburg, and of William HARTSHORN, Esq. in Alexandria: And in North-Carolina, under the management of James GALLAWAY, Esq. in Rockingham, of Robert BURTON, Esq. in Granville, of Allen JONES, Esq. in Halifax, of Hardy MURFREE, Esq. in Murfreesborough, of John HAMILTON, Esq. in Edenton, of Zedekiah STONE, Esq. in Windsor, and of Thomas HARVEY, Esq. in Nixonton... Test, Robert BROUGH, Clerk.

(226) For Sale. That valuable plantation, situate on the South-West bank of Chowan river, in Hertford county, called Petty Shore, containing 810 acres of Land...an excellent shad and herring fishery with commodious salt and packing houses, a dwelling house almost new..terms..will be made known by applying to Joseph A. BROWN, in Bertie county, James HATHAWAY, at Edenton, or the subscriber on the premises. Thomas BROWNRIGG. October 12th, 1796.

Vol. XI. THURSDAY, October 20, 1796. Numb. 561.

(227) From the New World. (A paper published in Philadelphia.) PEALE's New Patent Bridge... N. B. Those who desire to execute this method of bridge-building*, will please to apply to me..at the Museum, Philadelphia..to obtain drawings and estimates. C. W. PEALE. *The right of invention being secured by a patent agreeable to law.

(228) Denton (sic) (Edenton), October 20. To the Citizens of the Chowan District (composed of the lower counties of the District of Edenton) for the election of a President and Vice-President of the United States. Fellow Citizens, I beg leave to offer myself to you as an elector.. The candidates held forth in the prints, are, ADAMS, JEFFERSON and PINCKNEY. To ADAMS I am opposed, upon every ground which information hath stated to me. If elected, I shall vote for JEFFERSON... John HAMILTON. At Edenton Superior Court, October Term, 1796.

(229) Notice. Will be Sold, at Plymouth, on the 4th of November, a large quantity of West-India produce, the property of William ARMISTEAD, jun. deceased, consisting of Rum, Sugar, Molasses, Coffee and Salt..; and at the same time and place, will be sold, his Land, which lies in the counties of Beaufort, Tyrrell, Bertie and Franklin, and a number of lots in the town of Plymouth, among which are several water lots... The Executors. Plymouth, October 13, 1796.

(230) To the Citizens of Chowan, Tyrell, Gates, Perquimans, Currituck, Pasquotank, and Camden Counties. Gentlemen, I hereby offer you my services as a Candidate at the ensuing election for an elec-

(230) (Cont.) tor, to vote for a President and Vice-President of the United States. Thomas P. WILLIAMS

(231) State of North-Carolina. Chowan County, October 17, 1796. Notice is hereby given, to all the creditors of John BROWNRIGG, of the said county..is dead, and that the subscribers qualified as executors on the estate of the said deceased, in last October term... Thomas BROWNRIGG, Joseph A. BROWN, Ex'rs.

Vol. XI. THURSDAY, October 27, 1796. Numb. 562.

(232) Edenton, October 27. Died, on the 10th inst. at New-York, after a lingering illness, Mr. Robert EGAN, of this town.

(233) On the 24th of July last, Mr. John HARWOOD, and English gentleman, arrived at this place, in the schooner Payne, Capt. John MANN, from Philadelphia; Any person who can inform the subscriber what is become of..Mr. HARWOOD, will render the most essential service to the friends of that gentleman... Nathaniel ALLEN. Edenton, Oct. 25, 1796.

(234) Wishing in future to close my accounts annually, all persons indebted, are respectfully solicited to make payment. Gabriel N. PHILLIPS. Edenton, October 26, 1796.

(235) Thomas B. LITTLEJOHN and Co. Have just imported from New-York, a general assortment of Dry Goods... Edenton, October 24, 1796.

(236) The subscriber has just imported from New York..a general assortment of Dry Goods..and has also furnished his store at the wharf, with..Grocery and Ship Chandlery Goods, which he intends continuing in future, as a Grocery and Ship Chandlery Store, Entirely. William LITTLEJOHN. Edenton, October 24, 1796.

Vol. XI. THURSDAY, November 3, 1796. Numb. 563.

(237) Edenton, November 3. Supervisor's Office. There has appeared in..the district of North Carolina, a disposition among some distillers of native materials, to..employ two stills... William POLK, Supervisor of the Revenue, District of North Carolina. October 4, 1796.

Vol. XI. THURSDAY, November 10, 1796. Numb. 564.

(238) Edenton, November 10. Henry WILLS, Has just received from New-York, a fresh supply of Fall Goods..and for sale, Port and Sherry Wine, French Brandy, Holland Geneva, Brown Stout, Porter...

(239) Henderson STANDIN, Has just received from New-York, and opening at his store next to Mr. MARE's, an assortment of Dry Goods.. Edenton, Nov. 8, 1796.

Vol. XI. THURSDAY, November 17, 1796. Numb. 565.

(240) Baltimore, November 2. American Claims In the High Court of

(240) (Cont.) Admiralty. Sir James MARRIOT, Judge, ___ ___, agent to the United States, &c. in behalf of Messrs. John and Thomas STEPHENS, and Israel THORNDIKE, citizens of the United States, and owners of the schooner Relief and cargo, Asia COLE, master; Claimants against General Sir Charles GREY, and Admiral Sir John JARVIS...

(241) Richmond, November 9. To the People of the United States. I am informed that some citizens wish to vote for me at the ensuing election, to be President of the United States. I give them my thanks..But..publickly..declare..to decline, because of my inability to discharge the duties of it in a proper manner. Patrick HENRY. November 3d, 1796.

(242) Edenton, November 17. John HAMILTON, Esq. is chosen an elector for Edenton division, to vote for a President and Vice-President of the United States.

(243) State of North-Carolina. Chowan county, Nov. 14, 1796. Notice is hereby given, to all the creditors of John Joseph COMBS, of Tyrrell county..is dead, and that the subscriber qualified as administrator to the estate of the said deceased, at the last term of Tyrell court... Thomas B. LITTLEJOHN, Adm.

Vol. XI.   THURSDAY, November 24, 1796.   Numb. 566.

(244) Boston, October 31. Longevity. "Chester, October 17, 1796. The Rev. Mr. FLAGG, of this town, was born in 1704, graduated at Harvard College, in 1725, and is the oldest clergyman in the catalogue.. He retains his mental faculties unimpaired; hears and sees well, and reads with great pleasure..."

(245) To Mariners. On the 10th inst. the light-house, dwelling-house, &c. on the island of Sequin (?) (at the mouth of Kennebeck river) was completed. They were built under the direction of the Honourable Henry DEARBORN...

(246) New-York, November 9. Yesterday at 2 o'clock, the Senate and the Assembly chose the following gentlemen electors for this state, of President and Vice-President..Lewis MORRIS, West-Chester. Abijah HAMMOND, New-York. Richard THORNE, Queen's. Peter CANTINE, jun., Dutchess. Robert VAN RENSSELAER, Columbia. Abraham TEN BROECK, Albany. William ROOT, Rensselaer. Charles NEWKIRK, Montgomery. Abraham VAN VECHTEN, Albany. Johannes MILLER, Ulster. John HONEYWOOD, Washington. Peter SMITH, Herkemer. The above named gentlemen compose the Federal ticket.

(247) Elizabeth-Town, Nov. 9. At a joint meeting of the Council and assembly of this state, on the 3d inst. the following appointments were made. John RUTHERFORD, re-elected Senator of the United States. Electors of President and Vice-President.. Aron OGDEN, Essex. John NELSON, Middlesex. Elisha LAWRENCE, Monmouth. Caleb NEWBOLD, Burlington. Jonathan RHEA, Hunterdon. John BLACKWOOD, Gloucester. William COLEFAX, Bergen.

(248) Philadelphia, Nov. 5. We stop the press to give the result of the election in this city for Electors. For JEFFERSON Ticket, headed by Thomas M'KEAN, 1733. For ADAMS Ticket, headed by I. WARREN (?), 1091.

(249) Nov. 10. By the proclamation of the Governor of Maryland, of the 2d inst. it appears that the following gentlemen are elected members of the __ Congress for that state, viz., George DENT, Richard SPRIGG, Wm. CRAICK, George BAER, Samuel SMITH, William MAT__ES, William HINDMAN, and John DENNIS.

(250) Edenton, November 24. Joseph DAKINGS and Co. Inform..that they have received, of their own importations from Europe..Dry Goods.

(251) New Store. Edenton, Nov. 23, 1796. C. W. JANSON, From Boston, Has this day, by the arrival of the brig Commerce, been enabled to complete his stock of new Goods.. N. B. The above Goods are, for the present, stored in the house lately occupied by Capt. Stephen CARPENTER, opposite Mr. MOODY's wholesale store, where they will be sold...

Vol. XI. THURSDAY, December 1, 1796. Numb. 567.

(252) Philadelphia, Nov. 9. Copy of a letter from Dr. Edward MILLER, to Benjamin WYNKOOP, on the subject of a patent Machine for expelling foul air from the holds of ships at sea. "New York, 15th October, 1796...In my inspection of your machine, I was accompanied by my learned friend Dr. L. S. MITCHEL, professor of chemistry in the college of this city..." Edward MILLER.

Vol. XI. THURSDAY, December 8, 1796. Numb. 568.

(253) New-York, November 10. On Thursday evening last, about 6 o'clock, a fire broke out in a neat unfinished range of buildings in Reed-street.. We are informed that Mr. WILKINS, Mr. H. KIP, Mr. R. SNOW, and a Mr. SMITH are the principal sufferers.

(254) Edenton, December 8. Died, on Thursday night last, much lamented, Mrs. Ann BLOUNT, wife of Jacob BLOUNT, Esq. and daughter of Josiah COLLINS, Esq. of this town. Her remains were respectfully interred in the Church yard, on Saturday afternoon.

(255) Married on Tuesday night last, Capt. James HATHAWAY, to Miss Elizabeth VALENTINE, both of this town.

(256) Electors. William EDMUNDS is chosen an Elector to vote for a President and Vice-President..for the division of Northampton, &c. Sterling H_RWELL is chosen for the division of Halifax, &c. Anthony BROWN, is chosen for the division of Wake, &c. The Hon. R. D. SPAIGHT, is chosen for the division of Newbern, &c. John BRADLEY is chosen for the division of Wilmington.

(257) The Legislature of the state of Virginia, have appointed Patrick Henry, Esq. Governor of that state, in the room of Robert BROOK, Esq. who has accepted the appointment of Attorney-General.

(258) Martin SHEEL, Has just received from Baltimore, and opening at his store opposite Doctor RAMCKE's, in the house belonging to Mr. EELBECK, the Following Goods...

(259) Walter HUBBELL and Co. Inform the public that they have taken into partnership John WHEELER at Murfreesborough, where they propose carrying on their business under the firm of HUBBELL, WHEELER and Co... Windsor, Nov. 1st, 1796.

Vol. XI. THURSDAY, December 15, 1796. Numb 569.

(260) Boston, November 21. British Amity. The subscriber sailed from Boston, 22d February last, for Liverpool, and from thence for Philadelphia, in the ship Andrastus of Kennebeck. Off George's Bank, was brought to by the Assistance, British 50 gun ship; took out 5 hands, kept 2 of us and sent 3 back; we shewed our protections signed by the British Consul, but the officers tore them up and stamped on them.. There was 23 Americans on board the Assistance.. on the night of the 15th October, lying in Hampton Roads, we plunged into the sea and swam 4 miles to shore... Charles HALL. Marshfield Nov. 16, 1796.

(261) Copy of a letter, from S. CARBOT, Esq. to Messrs. E. DAVIS and Son, of this town, (Boston) dated "London, Sept. 24, 1796..."

(262) New-York, November 26. The ship Lydia, Capt. GOODRICH, arrived at this port on Friday last, in 37 days from Lisbon. Mr. George POLLOCK, owner of the Lydia, informs...

(263) A proclamation has this day been __ the Governor, that Thomas M'KEAN, ___ MORGAN, James BOYD, Peter M___, Joseph HEISTER, William MACLEY, _____, John WHITEHILL, William IRVINE, Abraham (?) SMITH, John PIPER, John S___, William (?) BROWN, Robert COLEMAN, and ___ MILES, appears,..to be elected Electors of a President and Vice-President...

(264) Fredericksburg, Dec. 2. From Richmond, Extract from the Journal of the House of Delegates, of this Commonwealth, of Friday the 18th instant, Mr. Henry LEE reported...

(265) Edenton, December 15. We hear that at the balloting of our Electors for President and Vice-President of the United States, at Raleigh, the poll stood as follows: For WASHINGTON, 1, JEFFERSON, 11, ADAMS, 1, BURR, 6, James IREDELL, 3, Thos. PINCKNEY, 1, Chas. C. PINCKNEY, 1. Patrick HENRY having refused the office of Governor of the state of Virginia,..Gen. WOOD has been appointed.

(266) State of North-Carolina. Pasquotank county, Dec. 6, 1796. Notice is hereby given, to all the creditors of John SYMONS, of the county aforesaid..is dead, and that the subscriber qualified as administrator to the estate of said deceased, at the last term of Pasquotank court... John NIXON, Adm.

(267) Ten Dollars Reward. Made his escape, on the 16th instant, near Hertford, in Perquimans, my negro fellow JOB; he is about 5

(267) (Cont.) feet 6 inches high, rather black, has remarkable small feet and hands, 25 or 30 years of age; he was bred in Perquimans, and..may be lurking about there, as he has a mother and other relations not far from Hertford; he was one of the negroes emancipated by the Quakers, and taken up and sold by order of court... Thomas POOL. Pasquotank, Nov. 28, 1796.

(268) Stolen from the subscriber, in June last, a Cypress Canoe... Thomas Wm. THOMPSON. Chowan County near Edenton.

Vol. XI. THURSDAY, December 22, 1796. Numb. 563.

(269) President of the United States, to both Houses of Congress, December 7, 1796... The Commissioners appointed on the part of the United States and of Great Britain, to determine which is the river St. Croix..in the treaty of peace of 1783, agreed in the choice of Egbert BENSON, Esq. of New-York, for the third Commissioner. Other commissioners..relative to captures and condemnations of vessels and other property, met..in August, last when John TRUMBULL, Esq. was chosen by lot, for the fifth commissioner. G. WASHINGTON. United States, 7th Dec. 1796.

(270) Petersburg, Dec. 13. The Electors of President and Vice-President of the United States, met at the capitol, in the city of Richmond, on Wednesday the 7th instant, and voted as follows: For Thomas JEFFERSON, 20, Samuel ADAMS, 15, George CLINTON, 3, George WASHINGTON, 1, John ADAMS, 1, Thomas PINCKNEY, 1, Aaron BURR, 1 / 42.

(271) Edenton, December 22. State of North-Carolina. Perquimans county, Dec. 14, 1796. Notice is hereby given, to all the creditors of Joseph NORCOM, of the said county..is dead, and that the subscriber qualified as administrator on the estate of said deceased, in last December term... Frederick NORCOM, Adm.

(272) State of North-Carolina. Chowan County, Dec. 21, 1796. Notice is hereby given, that Robert EGAN, of the county aforesaid, and town of Edenton, is dead, and that the subscribers qualified as executors to the estate of said deceased according to law. John H. COATES, Allen RAMSAY, Exr's.

(273) State of North-Carolina. Pasquotank county, Dec. 8, 1796. Notice is hereby given to all the creditors of James DALGLISH, deceased, of the said county, is dead, and that the subscriber qualified as administrator on the estate of the said deceased... Reuben KEATON, Adm.

(274) Twenty Dollars Reward. Run Away from the subscriber, on the night of the 3d inst., a likely young negro fellow named JOHN, formerly the property of Col. Michael PAYNE, of Edenton; he is a smart sensible fellow and speaks good English, about 5 feet 8 or 9 inches high... James WOOD. Hertford, Dec. 10, 1796.

Vol. XI. THURSDAY, December 29, 1796. Numb. 564.

(275) Philadelphia, Dec. 20. Fire At New York! Letters from New York, 9th December, 1796, to the Editor. This morning at 1 o'clock, a fire broke out at Murray's wharf, below the Coffee House, and consumed the whole block of buildings from that Slip to the Fly-Market, about 50 or 60 in number. The principal sufferers are Robert BROWN, John MURRAY, John TAYLOR, John MARSTON, STEWART and JONES, ROBINSON and HARTSHORE, LOOMIS and TILLINGHAST, David G. HUBBARD, David WAGSTAFF, &c...

(276) Edenton, December 3__. Owing to the delay of the Post, occasioned by the intense cold weather experienced here some days past, we have been obliged to postpone the publication of the State Gazette to this day.

(277) William SMITH, John RUTLEDGE, jun., Lemuel BENSON, Thomas SUMLER (?), Robert Goodloe HARPER, and William SMITH, are chosen by the people of South Carolina, Representatives in Congress.

(278) The Hon. Samuel ASHE, Esq. is re-elected Governor of this State for the ensuing year. John HAYWOOD, Esq. Treasurer-John CRAVEN, Esq. Comptroller.

(279) Whereas my wife Mary, without any just cause of complaint hath eloped from my bed and board, all persons are therefore desired not to trust her on my account, as I am determined not to pay any debt she may contract after this date, unless she returns to her good behaviour. All persons are forewarned, at their peril, harbouring her. Michael M'KEEL. December 27th, 1796.

(280) Dismal Swamp Canal. We have appointed Robert BROUGH, Esq. to receive subscriptions for New Shares in the Dismal Swamp Canal, in the room of George KELLY, Esq. dec... Thomas WILLOCK, A. SLAUGHTER, and J. G. MARTIN, Directors. Norfolk, Dec. 3, 1796.

(281) Dismal Swamp Canal. At a Meeting of the Directors of the Dismal Swamp Canal Company, December 20, 1796. Ordered, That the holders of shares pay to James BOYCE, Esq. Treasurer, the further sum of Twenty-Five dollars on each share on or before the first day of February next;..the eighth requisition of the old stock, and the first of the new subscriptions... Teste, Robert BROUGH, Cl'k.

(282) The Subscriber has received, by the brig Jenny, from Philadelphia,..Bottled Porter and Port Wine... Nathaniel ALLEN. Edenton, December 9th, 1796. The large Ware House, at present occupied by the Messrs. BIXBY's, to be Let...

Vol. XI. THURSDAY, January 5, 1797. Numb. 572.

(283) ____ the ensuing General Assembly of the state of North Carolina, to be held at Raleigh, ____ remonstrance and petition of the people called Quakers, from their yearly meeting held in Pasquotank county,..1796.. Therefore we earnestly intreat and request, that you..pass an act whereby the free citizens of this state, who are concientiously scrupulous of holding slaves, may legally emancipate

(283) (Cont.) them and the persons so liberated be under protection of law... Levi MUNDEN, Clerk.

(284) New-York, Dec. 17, 1796. Serious Cause of Alarm.. It is a fact, that there is a combination of incendiaries in this city.. The house of Mr. Lewis OGDEN, in Pearl street, has been twice set on fire..and he has put his blackman suspected to prison.

(285) Rape. His Excellency Governor JAY has issued his Proclamation, dated 15th inst. conformable to law and an affidavit forwarded by Governor MIFFLIN of Pennsylvania, for the apprehension and commitment of one Samuel BANCROFT, who is charged with committing a rape on the body of a little girl of 8 years, named Fanny SIBBALD, at Philadelphia, in this present month of December. The villain who perpetrated the above horrid act, is a young man about 25 years old, remarkable handsome and genteel in his person, was born in London of an overgrown rich family, from which circumstance he is haughty, insolent and overbearing. Fifty Dollars will be left with the Sheriff of New-York.. The infant named in the proclamation it is supposed will not recover from the injury...

(286) Edenton, January 5. C. W. JANSEN, Has for Sale, at his store, nearly opposite the Court-House (lately occupied by Mr. Thomas SEAMAN) in Edenton..the following assortment of Goods...

(287) Advertisement. Will be Sold, at public auction, on Wednesday and Thursday, the 18th and 19th days of January next, at the dwelling house of the subscriber, his Stock of Cattle, and Sheep, one Horse and Farming Utensils..excellent Household and Kitchen Furniture. Will be sold on the same days, 40 or 50 valuable Lots, in the town of Coleraine... John CAMPBELL. Lazy-Hill, Dec. 20, 1796.

Vol. XII. THURSDAY, January 12, 1797. Numb. 573.

(288) New-York, Dec. 20. This morning..the board fence in the back yard of Mr. James HEARD, in William street was discovered to be on fire, but was easily extinguished. There are strong suspicions of intentional mischief.

(289) Norfolk, January 7. Capt. LILLIBRIDGE, on the 20th December in lat. 37, 4, long. 73, spoke the brig ___, Timothy RUSSELL, master, of Philadelphia, out __ days from St. Ubes, in great distress...

(290) Newbern, December 31. Died on Friday the 23d inst. in the city of Raleigh, the Hon. John LEIGH, Esq. Speaker of the House of Commons. On Saturday following, Mrs. Catharine HUNLEY, Consort of Capt. Richard HUNLEY, of this town. And on Wednesday last, James COOR, Esq. an old inhabitant of this town, formerly a member of the Legislature, and Speaker of the Senate.

(291) Edenton, January 12. Letters remaining in the Post-Office at Edenton, Jan. 1, 1797. John ARMISTEAD, Sarah ARMISTEAD, Joseph BONNER, John F. ASPRAY, Monsieur BREOL, Blake BAKER, Thomas BENT, John BALLARD, Peter BLACHON, Alexander BLACK, Jesse BALLARD, Wm.

(291) (Cont.) BLOUNT, John BORRITZ, James BAKER, Henry BAKER, Wm. CRAWFORD, Clerk of the county court of Chowan, John P. CASE, Mary CARY, Robert CUSHING, James CHEW, Anthony DAILETT, James FINCH, Madamoiselle GAUZAN, J. GOODWIN, Cha's. HAUGHTON, Frazer GRIFFIN, Wm. HILL, Benjamin HALL, Charles HUNT, John HALSEY, Capt. E. JONES, C. W. JANSON, Marmaduke JONES, Shobel KELLY, Patrick KELLY, Henry KENNEDY, James H. KEYS, James LOVE, Rebecca LONG, James M'KINLEY, Aaron MORRIS, Exum NEWBY, John PORTER, Christopher REED, Edward RUSSELL, Wm. RUMBOUGH, Martin SHEEL, Elizabeth SMITH, Isaac SILLIMAN, Wm. SUTTON, Capt. Daniel UDALL, Capt. Thomas WALKER, James WINTER, John OTIS, John WALLACE, Samuel WELLS, Hambleton WARRING, Samuel WHITING. Hend. STANDIN, A. P. M.

(292) Thomas B. LITTLEJOHN and Co. Have for Sale, A Small, but well assorted quantity of Dry Goods, Hardware and Crockery, which they will sell at whole sale only... Edenton, Jan. 10, 1797.

(293) At Edenton, on Tuesday, the 17th inst. will be hired out.. a number of Negroes..by the subscriber... Michael PAYNE. Edenton, Jan. 9, 1797.

(294) Alexandria, December 24. On Thursday evening the School House of Henry WALKER, of this town, was destroyed by fire...

(295) Patent Printing Press. We have..a small paper, entitled The New Star, printed for the purpose of making experiments, with a model of a Printing Press on a new plan, lately invented by Apollus KINSLEY, of Hertford, Conn. (Salem paper.)

Vol. XII. THURSDAY, January 19, 1797. Numb. 574.

(296) An act for improving the navigation of Roanoak river, from the town of Halifax, to a point or place which shall be one mile below the place where the Virginia line intersects the same.. I. Be it enacted by the General Assembly of the State of North Carolina ..That it shall..be lawful to open books of subscription at Halifax town, in Halifax county, North Carolina, under the management of Thomas AMIS, Willie JONES, Goodoram DAVIS, or any two of them; at Danville in Pittsylvania county, in Virginia, under the management of John WILSON, sen., Robert PAYNE and James COLQUHOUN, or any two of them; and at St. Tamaney in the county of Mecklenburg, in the state of Virginia..under the management of Samuel GOODE, Hume R. FIELD and Samuel HOPKINS, or any two of them; and at South Boston, in the county of Halifax, in the state of Virginia..under the management of George CARRINGTON, John B. SCOTT and Charles BRUCE, or any two of them, for receiving subscriptions to the amount of eighty thousand dollars for the said undertaking..subscribers, their heirs and assigns..are declared to be incorporated by and under the name of the Roanoak Navigation Company... Benjamin SMITH, S.S., M. MATTHEWS, S.H.C.

(297) Edenton, January 19. From the Pittsburg Gazette. Died, on Wednesday night, the 14th December, at Presqu Isle, His Excellency Anthony WAYNE, Commander in Chief of the Federal army.

(298) The House, lately occupied as a store by Mr. FEREBEAU, is for Sale..terms by enquiring of The Printer.

(299) State of North-Carolina. Pasquotank county, January 12. Notice is hereby given, to all the creditors of John TRUEBLOOD, of the said county,..is dead, and that the subscriber qualified as executor, on the estate of said deceased, in last December term... Benj. ALBERTSON, Ex'r.

(300) Notice. All persons indebted to the estate of John Joseph COMBES, dec...are requested to make immediate payment. For the convenience of those creditors living in Martin and Tyrrell, their accounts are lodged with John ARMISTEAD, Esq. at Plymouth... Thomas B. LITTLEJOHN, Adm. Edenton, January 14, 1797.

(301) John HORNIBLOW, Having purchased the Tavern, lately belonging to Robert EGAN, deceased, informs the public in general that he has opened said Tavern. His Plantation, on the Sound side, known by the name of Horniblow's Point, is hereby offered for sale..500 acres.

(302) For Sale, A Larg (sic) Upper Mill Stone, of a good quality, about five feet diameter, and one and a half foot thick. For terms apply to Richard HOSKINS. Edenton, Jan. 17, 1797.

(303) Notice. That on Wednesday, the 15th day of February next, will be Sold, at public vendue, before Mr. James WOOD's tavern, in the town of Hertford, one Plantation and Tract of Land, containing 385 acres, beautifully situated on Albemarle sound, in Perquimans county, with a creek running up on one side, which is a line between said land, and the land of Thomas WHEDBEE, and in one of the best places for fowling and fishing in this state. Also seven likely Young Negroes, the property of Joseph NORCOM, deceased. At the same time and place will be rented out, until the first day of January, 1798, the plantation whereon the said deceased lived. Chowan county, Jan. 11th, 1797.

Vol. XII. THURSDAY, January 26, 1797. Numb. 575.

(304) Norfolk, January 16. In the House of Representatives of the United States, on the 3d inst. Mr. W. SMITH, of the committee of ways and means, reported to the House...

(305) Edenton, January 26. January 20, 1797. Gentlemen, Agreeable to the annexed resolutions entered into by the inhabitants, convened at the court house on the 12th inst. we have made every enquiry.. into the origin of the late alarm, &..assure you, that no information has been given us to warrant the smallest apprehension of a conspiracy... Jacob BLOUNT, James GRANBERY. The Commissioners of Edenton. By order, Alex'r. MILLEN, Town Clerk.

(306) State of North-Carolina. Pasquotank county, Jan. 12. Notice is hereby given, to all the creditors of John ROWAN, of the said county,..is dead, and that the subscriber qualified as administrator on the estate of the said deceased, in last December term... Timothy TRUEBLOOD, Adm.

(307) From an unexpected situation of my affairs in New-York, my return becomes absolutely necessary... G. N. PHILLIPS.

(308) Doctor John CUNNINGHAM, Informs the inhabitants of Edenton.. that he has for Sale, at his house, (at the upper end of Broad street for the present) a choice parcel of genuine Drugs and Medicines... Edenton, Jan. 24, 1797.

Vol. XII. THURSDAY, February 2, 1797. Numb. 576.

(309) Philadelphia, Jan. 12. On Monday the dwelling house of Elias BOUDINOT, Esq. of Newark (New Jersey) caught Fire, and was entirely consumed.

(310) At a meeting of the American Philosophical Society, Thomas JEFFERSON was elected President in the room of David RITTENHOUSE, deceased.

(311) Savannah, January 13. "On Monday night last, an attempt was made to set fire to the house of John BERR__, Esq. but fortunately discovered it in time to prevent its effects. And on Thursday night a fire was placed among some shavings under the store of Mr. POSNER, but was extinguished without any material injury."

(312) Norfolk, January 26. Yesterday arrived here the brig Betsey, Captain Timothy BAKER, 21 days from St. Martins.. Ship Sally, of New York, Captain John B_E, from Demarara, bound home-vessel and cargo condemned. Left There. Capt. BAKER also informs, that the American Indiaman, the Ru_id_ek, of Providence (R. I.) Capt. J. ABORN, from the Isle of France, was captured by a French cruiser on the 26th of December, and carried into St. Martin's.. Came passenger in the brig Betsey, Captain John HALL, of the schooner Rebecca of Baltimore...

(313) Yesterday arrived the schooner Barbara, Capt. Joseph WHITE, jun. in 18 days from the Havanna...

(314) Jan. 21. Spoke the schooner Success, of Beverly, Capt. FOSTER, 55 days out..had fallen in with the brig Thomas, Capt. Israel DONE (?), then 75 days out from Jamaica; and the sloop Nancy, Captain Isaac ESTICK, from Antigua for Baltimore; both of which Capt. F. supplied with provisions. They had lost two hands.

(315) Edenton, February 2. From a Correspondent. The descendants of Mrs. Sarah BLOUNT of Chowan county, near Edenton, now living and enjoying a good state of health, are 8 children, 75 grand children, and 56 great grand children, in all 139.

(316) Taken by execution, and will be Sold, on Wednesday, the 15th of March next, on the premises..one half the Wharf, Ware Houses, and Water Lots, belonging thereunto, now occupied by Mr. Thomas B. LITTLEJOHN, to satisfy a judgement obtained by the executors of Edward KERR, against Myles O'MALLEY, administrator to the estate of Matthew O'MALLEY, deceased. Michael PAYNE, Marshal. Edenton, January 30, 1797.

Vol. XII. THURSDAY, February 9, 1797. Numb. 577.

(317) Notice. All persons indebted..to the concerns of YOUNG, MILLER, and Co. and ALSTON, YOUNG and Co., at their stores in Edenton, Tyrrell, Halifax, Granville, Hillsborough, or Guilford, are requested to come to an immediate Settlement... Those indebted at their stores in Edenton and Tyrrell, will be pleased to settle ..with William LITTLEJOHN, in Edenton; those..in Halifax, with Mr. Starling MARSHALL, merchant there;..in Granville, Hillsborough and Guilford, (for the present) with Mr. George ALSTON, merchant, Granville... William LITTLEJOHN, George ALSTON, Surviving Partners in America. February 6, 1797.

(318) The subscribers have remaining on hand, about 1200 bushels of Cadiz Salt, laying in the town of Edenton, which they will sell low, for cash, or short credit. Walter HUBBELL, and Co. Windsor, Feb. 8, 1797.

(319) Baltimore, January 10. At a meeting in the usual manner of the Old Fielders, on Tuesday evening the 3d inst. (the anniversary of the battle of Princeton, won by Old Fielder George WASHINGTON, in 1777) William JESSUP in the chair, (Henry STEVENSON being indisposed) the following toasts were drank by friendly brethren: (To) George WASHINGTON, John ADAMS, Thomas JEFFERSON, Thomas PINCKNEY, Aaron BURR, The memory of Anthony WAYNE, John Egor HOWARD, Daniel MORGAN, and William WASHINGTON.

Vol. XII. THURSDAY, February 16, 1797. Numb. 578.

(320) Bermuda, January 7. Saturday last the brig Three Brothers, Geo. BROWN, master, of and from New-Haven in Connecticut, run on the rocks on the West End, and knocked her rudder off..she is totally lost...

(321) Salem, January 20. By the schooner Raven, Captain Ambrose MARTIN, which arrived at Marblehead on Monday evening last, in 38 days from St. Eustatia.. On the 4th of December..Capt. Benjamin DIAMOND, in a sloop belonging to Salem, that very morning carried in by a French privateer, being bound to Antigua from Charleston ..was wantonly run down by one of the British ships of war, and his mate, one sailor and a black and a white boy, were drowned, and the vessel and cargo entirely lost.

(322) Philadelphia, Jan. 27. Melancholy and Distressing. This morning about a quarter before 6 o'clock, a fire broke out in the lower part of the dwelling house of Mr. Andrew BROWN, printer of this city.. Mr. BROWN is very much burnt, and is dangerously ill. Mrs. BROWN and her three children, a son and two daughters, fell victim to the flames and suffocation.

(323) Jan. 30. Another Fire. Broke out Saturday evening in the Malt (?) Room of Mr. Thomas MORRIS's Brewhouse-Moravian alley. On Saturday the remains of Mrs. BROWN and her three children (the eldest a girl of 13, the second a boy of 9 and the youngest a girl of 7 years of age) were conveyed in three coffins from the house

(323) (Cont.) of Major Robert PATTON, to the grave yard of St. Paul's Church.. Mr. BROWN..is now out of danger.. We hear that the Philadelphia Gazette will be continued by Mr. CAREY, Mr. BROWN's assistant...

(324) Norfolk, February 6. William COBBETT of Philadelphia has issued proposals for publishing a daily paper in that city, under the title of "Porcupine Gazette".

(325) Edenton, February 16. Extract of a letter from Washington, to a gentleman in Newbern, Feb. 7. This evening arrived at this place, in 15 days from Cape Francois, Captain T. SMITH, late master of the brig Russel of this port...

(326) For Sale, A Philadelphia made Double Chair, with a top. For terms apply to Thomas SEAMAN.

(327) From the Baltimore Telegraphe. Messrs. CLAYLAND, DOBBIN & Co. I Have just been presented with the enclosed letters, and sent you a copy (the originals are in the hands of Mr. James CALHOUN)... Your's &c. Joshua BARNEY, Brigadier-General in the service of France. Baltimore, Jan. 20. Charleston, Jan. 3, 1797. James CALHOUN, Esq.... (Signed) W. & E. CRAFFTS. At Sea, 12th December 1796. Sir, Having met the schooner Sally, bound to Charleston, Captain John LEICH... (Signed) L'EVEILLE, Merchant, Baltimore.

Vol. XII. THURSDAY, February 23, 1797. Numb. 579.

(328) Nassau, (N. P.) Jan. 24. Yesterday the Bermudian privateer Fortune of War, Capt. ADAMS, came in with a recaptured American schooner named the Venus, of Charleston, George M. HAFFORD (or HASSARD), master, from Port-au-Prince for Charleston, with a cargo of sugar.

(329) Philadelphia, Feb. 4..Feb. 6. The mournful catastrophe which has lately overwhelmed the family of Mr. BROWN..attained its full height on Saturday morning, by the death of Mr. BROWN, himself. The remains of Mr. BROWN were interred yesterday morning near those of his family in St. Paul's grave yard.

(330) Philadelphia, Feb. 9. Yesterday at 12 o'clock the two houses of Congress met in the Representatives' Chamber, when the President of the senate..opened and counted the votes of the several states for President and Vice-President.. The President of the Senate hereupon proclaimed John ADAMS, President of the United States, and Thomas JEFFERSON, Vice-President, for four years; from the 4th of March...

(331) Fayetteville, February 4. On the 16th ult. Mr. and Mrs. CLARE, of Robeson, was murdered by a mulatto girl...

(332) Edenton, February 23. Samuel ADAMS, Governor of Massachusetts, has declined being re-elected...

(333) For Sale. The complete Machinery, of a double gear Mill,

(333) (Cont.) the Stones are of an excellent quality, the whole appendages entirely new, and may be moved without difficulty. John HAMILTON.

Vol. XII. THURSDAY, March 2, 1797. Numb. 580.

(334) Edenton, March 2. Advertisement. All whom it may concern, are hereby informed of the death of Zedekiah STONE, of Bertie county, and that the subscriber has qualified as his executor... David STONE. Windsor, Feb. 14, 1796 (sic).

Vol. XII. THURSDAY, March 9, 1797. Numb. 581.

(335) New-York, Feb. 21. Messrs. M'LEAN & LANG,... The brig Susan and Polly, belonging to myself, Leffert LEFFERTS, and Thomas CARPENTER, has been taken on the 20th January on her way to Jamaica from this port, carried into Port-de-Pais and vessel and cargo condemned ... James M'INTOSH.

(336) New-York, February 22. Extract of a letter from Sam. BAYARD, Esq. to the Chairman of the Committee of Merchants of this city, dated London, November 25...

(337) Wilmington, Feb. 23. Extract of a letter from Capt. Benjamin GARDNER, to his owners in this town, dated Cape Nichola Mole, January 24. "A brig belonging to John BLOUNT, of Washington, from New Providence, bound to Jamaica, taken..totally condemned." Friday last arrived here the schooner Robinson Crusoe, Thomas C. CHURCH, left Barbadoes the 17th January..the day after was taken by a French privateer schooner called Reancy, Captain Bostin NEVARRE.. The schooner Two Brothers, Captain Jonathan GLOVER, from this port, was cast away on New-Topsail Inlet, the 10th inst. vessel and cargo lost, and Captain GLOVER's father drowned in attempting to swim to shore-fortunately the rest of the crew were saved.

(338) Norfolk, February 27. In the Supreme court of the United States, Monday February 13, 1797... Jacob WAGNER, Cl'k. Sup. Ct. U. S.

(339) Edenton, March 9. Perquimans County, February Term at Hertford, 1797. This certifies that it was then and there ordered, That the business of this court be hereafter arranged and distributed in the following manner... Test, John HARVEY, Clerk.

(340) Notice. All persons indebted to the estate of Robert EGAN, deceased..are informed, That Mr. Thomas GORDON will attend here, for Mr. John H. COATES, the second Monday in March, and continue one week, for the purpose of adjusting the accounts. Allen RAMSAY, Ex'r. February 25, 1797.

(341) Advertisement. Stolen away from the subscriber, at Mrs. CASTEN's, in Gates county, on Sunday the 26th ultimo, a Sorrel Mare ..reward of Fifteen Dollars.. Willis WOODLEY. March 2, 1797.

Vol. XII. THURSDAY, March 16, 1797. Numb. 582.

(342) Edenton, March 16. Just received From Cadiz, and for Sale by the Subscriber, a quantity of Salt and Sherry Wine. John LITTLE. March 15, 1797.

(343) Dismal Swamp Canal. At a meeting of the Directors of the Dismal Swamp Canal Company, February 20th, 1797. Ordered, That all those shares, which shall on the first day of May next be delinquent for any payment..required, be on that day, Sold at auction, before the Eagle Tavern, in the Borough of Norfolk... Robert BROUGH, Cl'k.

(344) State of North-Carolina. Pasquotank county, March 12th 1797. Notice is hereby given, to all whom it may concern, that Frederick PENDLETON, of the county aforesaid, is dead; and that the subscriber qualified as Executor to the last will and testament of the said deceased, at the last court. William T. MUSE.

Vol. XII. THURSDAY, March 23, 1797. Numb. 583.

(345) Boston, February 27. On Saturday morning, at nine o'clock, a fire broke out in the tar house belonging to Messrs. TYLER and CASWEL's rope manufactory..consumed three large rope-walks, at West Boston, the usual out buildings, four dwelling houses, and a barn. The rope-walks were owned by Messrs. RUSSEL and JEFFRY, John WINTHROP, Esq. and Messrs. TYLER and CASWEL... Messrs. TYLER and CASWEL lost nearly all, cordage, &c. besides about 50 tons of hemp, belonging to Mr. FORRESTER, of Salem. The dwelling houses owned by Joseph BAKER, jun. Esq. who saved a part of his furniture, Mr. William TYLER, rope maker, Mr. Nathaniel NARCROSS, carpenter, and Mr. Samuel NARCROSS, painter, Mr. John ANKERS, baker, and Messrs. ROBERTS and HUFFINS...

(346) New York, March 6. Spoliation. At a meeting of the underwriters in this city, affected by spoliations on American commerce, held at the Tontine Coffee-House, on Friday the 24th of February, Messrs. William NEILSON, Isaac GOUVERNEUR, and John B. COLES, were appointed a committee for the purpose of adopting such measures as they may deem necessary, for obtaining compensation for vessels and cargoes, with authority to employ an agent at the expence of the underwriters. The committee..have appointed Mr. John FERRERS as their agent...

(347) Edenton, March 23. Thomas SEAMAN, Having lately employed a Silver-Smith and jeweller, an excellent workman...

(348) Run away from the subscriber, living in Hyde county, a young negro fellow, of about 17 or 18 years of age, rather low stature, is black..his proper name is ABEL, though he frequently passes by the name of ABRAM; he has very lately been taken up, and was in possession of one Jethro PINDAR, near Murfreesborough, for a few days..escaped from him..he was 10 or 12 years ago brought from the eastern shore of Maryland, and was bought in Hyde by Col. Benjamin PARMERLE, and now is the property of the orphan son of that man, hired by me for the present year. J. ALDERSON. N. B. A line addressed to me by post to Washington, will reach me readily. March 16, 1797.

Vol. XII. THURSDAY, March 30, 1797. Numb. 584.

(349) Edenton, March 30. List of Acts passed at the second session of the fourth Congress, begun and held in the city of Philadelphia, on Monday the fifth day of December, 1796. ..Granting a certain sum of money to the widow and children of John DE NEUFVILLE, deceased.. For the remission of the duties of tonnage on the vessels of James O'BRIEN and James AYLWARD.

(350) Robert MOODY Informs the public, that he has formed a connection in business with John AVERY, jun. of Boston-that they will carry on business under the firm of MOODY and AVERY... Edenton, March 29th, 1797.

(351) Notice. That the noted, full-bred running horse Ugly, now the property of Col. BYNUM, of Virginia, will stand at Mr. Josiah REDDITT's, in Bertie county, on the main road leading from Edenton to Windsor.. Ugly..was got by the noted imported running horse Brilliant, and bred by Gen. SUMPTER, of South-Carolina; his dam is a thoroughbred mare, bred by Col. DANDRAGE, of Virginia... James TURNER.

Vol. XII. THURSDAY, April 6, 1797. Numb. 585.

(352) Norfolk, March 30. John DAWSON, Esq. is elected for the district of Orange, in the room of James MADISON, Esq. resigned. Anthony NEW, Esq. is re-elected for the district of Caroline. John CROPTON, Esq. is re-elected for the district of Henrico.

(353) Edenton, April 6. Taken by execution, and will be sold for ready money..on the premises, on Friday, the 19th day of May next, that valuable Tract of Land, containing 700 acres, on the southwest side of Pasquotank river, near the head..to Luke STALLION's line, in Perquimans county, agreeable to the patent.. The said land belonging to the estate of Matthew O'MALLEY, dec. and sold to satisfy a judgement obtained by the executors of Edward KERR, dec. against Myles O'MALLEY, administrator to Matthew O'MALLEY, deceased. Michael PAYNE, Marshal. North-Carolina District. Edenton, April 1st, 1797.

(354) Just received from New-York, in the schooner Penelope, A Small Assortment of Spring Goods... John VAIL. April 4, 1797.

(355) I regret the necessity of having to solicit a second time those indebted to make payment. Expecting to leave this state in a few days, I hope the present notice will be attended to immediately. G. N. PHILLIPS.

(356) Fifteen Dollars Reward. Run away from the subscriber, on the 17th ult. a negro man named SIMON, about 18 years old; he is of a dark complexion, about 4 feet 10 inches high, stout made... Joshua HAYES. Bertie county, April 2d, 1797.

Vol. XII. THURSDAY, April 13, 1797. Numb. 586.

(357) Edenton, April 13. By the President of the United States of America. A Proclamation. Whereas..I do by these presents convene the Congress of the United States of America, at the city of Philadelphia, in the commonwealth of Pennsylvania, on Monday, the 15th day of May next... John ADAMS. By the President, T. PICKERING, Secretary of State.

(358) State of North-Carolina. Hertford county, March 24th, 1797. Notice is hereby given, to all whom it may concern, that Edward MOORE, of the county aforesaid is dead, and that the subscriber qualified as executor to the last will and testament of the said deceased, at last May court... Jesse WILLIAMS.

Vol. XII. THURSDAY, April 20, 1797. Numb. 587.

(359) Edenton, April 20. John M'FARLANE, Physician and Surgeon, wishing to establish himself in Edenton, offers his services to the public, in the line of his profession.. He occupies the shop opposite to Mr. O'MALLEY's, lately held by Dr. PHILLIPS. Edenton, April 11, 1797.

(360) State of North-Carolina. Pasquotank county, April 11, 1797. Notice is hereby given, to all the creditors of Mary FARROW, of the said county..is dead, and that the subscriber qualified as administrator, on the estate of said deceased, in last March term... Joseph READING, Adm.

(361) State of North-Carolina. Pasquotank county, April 12, 1797. Notice is hereby given, to all the creditors of Aaron MORRIS, sen., of the said county..is dead, and that the subscriber qualified as executor to the estate of said deceased, in last December term... Joseph READING, Ex'r.

Vol. XII. THURSDAY, April 27, 1797. Numb. 588.

(362) Philadelphia, April 11. The following paper has this moment been handed to me and I think it of importance enough to stop the press in order to communicate it to the public. Wm. COBBETT... George WILSON, sen...

(363) Baltimore, April 15. Interesting Communication. London, Feb. 12, 1797. Mess. E. DAVIS and Son, Inclosed..an extract from the minutes of the commissioners in the case of the Betsey, Capt. FURLONG, owned by Messrs. PATTERSONS, of Baltimore... I am, &c. S. CABOT.

(364) Edenton, April 27. Letters remaining in the Post-Office at Edenton, April 1, 1797. John F. ASPRAY, Elisha ASHBURN, Nicholas ATKINS, Gen. Lawrence BAKER, John BROWN, Hezekiah BROADWELL, Mrs. S. BATES, Capt. Onan BERRY, Demsey BURGES, James BAKER, William BLOUNT, Martha BRITH, John BULLOCK, Michael CAPEHART, James CARMER, Capt. John COX, John H. COATES, Samuel R. CLARKSON, Gideon CORNELL, Sally CARTER, James CAMPBELL, John COWPER, Clerk of the Chowan court, Robert CUSHING, Ralph and E. CHAMBERLAIN, John DEVEREUX, John FRAZOR, Capt. Alexander FERGUSON, John GOELET, Josiah GRANBERY,

(364) (Cont.) Jonathan GOODWIN, Edward GILES, Capt. Joseph GOOLD, Capt. George HAZARD, Mary HAMMON, Thomas HANKINS, Lewis HUNTER, Henry LEE, William LEWIS, James LOVE, Malcolm M'COLM, Duncan M'DONALD, Isabella M'NIEL, David CLARK, Exum NEWBY, John NORCOM, jun., Frederic NASH, Myles O'MALLEY, Peter O'NEAL, Francis PEYRINNAUT, F. SPERIMENTS, Charles PETTIGREW, Solomon PENDAR, Cornelius S. QUIGLEY, Dr. Frederick RAMCKE, Henry RODNEY, Edward RILEY, David RIDDICK, Mary ROSS, Christian REED, Eliza SMITH, James SAUNDERS, Malachi SAWYER, Roger STONS, Granville SMITH, Samuel STREET, John SIMPSON, Thomas SHARROCK, Benjamin RICE, Thomas TROTTER, Capt. Thomas WALKERS, Capt. Thomas WHITE, WYNNS and BRICKLE, Dr. Ephraim WHITEMORE, Penelope WYNNES, Dr. Amos WINDSHIP, Capt. John WEADON, Capt. James WILLIAMS. Hend. STANDIN, P. M.

(365) State of North-Carolina. Pasquotank county, April 20, 1797. Notice is hereby given, to all whom it may concern, that Timothy PENDLETON, Asa WILLIAMS, and Noah PERKINS, of the county aforesaid are dead, and that the subscriber qualified as administrator to their several estates, at the last March court... Reuben KEATON, Adm.

(366) State of North-Carolina. Pasquotank county, April 20, 1797. Notice is hereby given, to all whom it may concern, that Samuel WHEDBEE, of the county aforesaid, is dead, and that the subscriber qualified as administrator with the will annexed to the estate of the said deceased, at the last March court... Reuben KEATON, Adm.

(367) Run away from the subscriber, in Northampton county, about 4 miles from Murfreesborough, on the night of the 6th instant, a negro boy by the name of JIM, about 19 years of age; he is slim made and very yellow.. He is about 5 feet 7 or 8 inches high... Ten Dollars reward... Arthur WILLIAMS, April 8, 1797.

Vol. XII. THURSDAY, May 3, 1797. Numb. 589.

(368) New-York, April 14. Capt. VAN RENSELLAER, late of the Schooner Two Friends, of this port, and belonging to Thomas WHITE, merchant of this city, came passenger in the Betsey.. The ship Eliza, Capt. ALLEN, of this port, belonging to Theophilus BROWER, merchant, was taken on his passage from Leogane to New-York..by the British sloop of war Albicore, Capt. FOSTER, and sent into Cape Nichola Mole.

(369) Edenton, May 4. Samuel WILLIAMS, Esq. merchant, of Boston, was, in July 1796, appointed Consul of the United States, for the city of Hamburgh.

(370) Mr. GREENLEAF, of New-York, printer of the Argus, has been tried before the circuit court of the United States, for a libel, of which he was pronounced guilty, and fined by the court (in which Judge ELLSWORTH sat as supreme) 700 dollars... The prosecutor, we understand was Sir John TEMPLE, the British Consul.

(371) The subscriber has for Sale, at the store of Messrs. E. and B. NORFLEET, a handsome assortment of tamboured muslins, muslin

(371) (Cont.) aprons and handkerchiefs, and a few diaper table cloths... Robert MORRIS. Edenton, May 1st, 1797.

(372) Forty Dollars Reward. Ran away from the subscriber on Saturday night, the 25th March, an apprentice boy named James HARRIS, (but who says he intended altering his name.) He is of a swarthy complexion, has a fat bloated face, a remarkable thick bushy head of strait dark hair; he is about 5 feet one and a half inches high, between 18 and 19 years of age.. It is probable that he may try to get with some Blacksmith, Carpenter, Cabinet-maker or Turner, as he is a tolerable good hand at either... Leven DORSEY. Norfolk, March 27, 1797.

Vol. XII. THURSDAY, May 11, 1797. Numb. 590.

(373) Philadelphia, April 14. Circuit Court of the United States for the Pennsylvania District. The Grand Inquest have listened to the Charge, this day delivered by the Court, with much pleasure.. a copy, for the purpose of making it known to the public.. J. COW-PERTHWAIT, F. M. April 11, 1797. A Charge. Delivered to the Grand Jury..April 11, 1797. By James IREDELL, one of the Associate Justices of the Supreme Court of the United States...

(374) Philadelphia, April 27. On Monday last Francis BILLATO, a citizen of the United States, was committed to the gaol of this city..for a misdemeanor, in entering on board a French privateer.. and also for treason, in levying war against the United States, by capturing on the high seas a vessel or vessels belonging to the citizens of the United States.

(375) Charleston, April 19. On Monday arrived in the brig Amsterdam, Mr. William RUTLEDGE from Amsterdam. On the 26th of February, he was at the Holder; he there saw Mr. Sylvanus BOURNE, the Consul of the United States.

(376) Edenton, May 11. Ten Dollars Reward. Run away, on the 3d of April, at night, a negro fellow named HARRY, about 5 feet 8 inches high, very black, has formerly worked at the shoemaking business, and can work at the black-smith's business... Nathan SKINNER. Perquimans county, Yaupim-creek. May 4th, 1797.

Vol. XII. THURSDAY, May 18, 1797. Numb. 591.

(377) Poughkeepsie, April 12. A foot race of 25 miles was run in three hours and fifty five minutes by a young man of the name of John SHREEVE, on Thursday the 10th inst. round the place called the Square, lying partly in Stanford and partly in Amenia. The young man won a prize of ten pounds...

(378) Norfolk, May 11. Captain Joseph RICHARDSON of the schooner Sally, of Philadelphia, sailed from Port-au-Prince the 23d of April..

(379) Norfolk, May 13. Extract of a letter from Jean RABEL, to a mercantile gentleman in this town, dated April 24...

(380) Edenton, May 18. MOODY and AVERY, Have for Sale, An assortment of European and India Goods, suitable for the present season ... Edenton, May 8th, 1797.

(381) To Be Sold, At private Sale, The House lately occupied by Mr. SIGAUD, next door to Mr. C. W. JANSON's, formerly belonging to Francis PORIE..enquire of the printer.

Vol. XII.   THURSDAY, May 25, 1797.   Numb. 592.

(382) Boston, May 5. Extract of a letter from Capt. John CRUFT, of the Barque Pomona, of this port, dated Malaga, March 12...

(383) Philadelphia, May 11. Launch of the United States 44 gun frigate. This superb vessel constructed by Joshua HUMPHREYS, under the inspection of her commander Captain John BARRY, in a style superior to any European vessel of equal size, the first built in America since the completion of our revolution-the first born of our navy-attracted to view her launch at least 40,000 spectators.. The frigate being safely moored in the Delaware under the direction of Captain Richard DALE who commanded on the occasion...

(384) Edenton, May 25. At the house of John HAMILTON, Esq. near Edenton, on the 21st instant, departed this life, William CUMMING, Esq. Attorney at law, a man of eminence in his profession, and of the greatest philanthropy.

(385) Died-at Quincey, Mrs. HALL, mother of his Excellency John ADAMS, President of the United States.

(386) Just received from New-York, And for Sale, by Jeremiah GALLOP, An assortment of Dry Goods and Groceries, &c...

(387) The partnership between John SHAW and STUART and BARR, trading at Nixonton, under the firm of John SHAW and Co. is dissolved by mutual consent. John SHAW, STUART & BARR. May 16, 1797.

(388) Baltimore, April 24. Horrid-Horrid Murder!!! At the General Court, for the Eastern Shore, now sitting, a negro woman, the property of Mr. ECCLESTON, of Kent county, in this state, was found guilty of the murder of a child of one of her fellow slaves.. by means of laudanum.. She has, since her condemnation, acknowledged to have destroyed, by poison, three children of Robert DUNN, Esq...of Kent...

Vol. XII.   THURSDAY, June 1, 1797.   Numb. 593.

(389) Congress. House of Representatives. Thursday, May 19... letters from Mr. John Quincy ADAMS, Ambassador in Batavia...

(390) Edenton, June 1. Notice. Will be sold, on Saturday the first day of July next, at Winton, for ready money, 10 or 12 likely country born Negroes..the property of Ebenezer GORHAM, sold by the subscriber, as Attorney for him. Lawrence BAKER. May 24th, 1797.

(391) Dismal Swamp Canal. At a meeting of the Directors of the Dismal Swamp Canal Company, May 12th, 1797. Ordered, that the holders of shares pay to James BOYCE, Esq. Treasurer, on or before the first day of September next, the further sum of Thirty Dollars for each share; This being the ninth payment required on the old, and the second on the new shares... Teste, Robert BROUGH, Clerk.

Vol. XII. THURSDAY, June 8, 1797. Numb. 594.

(392) Norfolk, May 29. In the senate on Saturday, John Q. ADAMS, the President's eldest son, was nominated Minister Plenipotentiary to the court of Berlin.

(393) Edenton, June 8. Mackey's Creek, Tyrrell County. The subscribers have for Sale, at Mackey's Creek, a faithful, strong and well built vessel... Thomas WORLEY, Michael KING. June 6th, 1797.

(394) Notice. That whereas there are 200,000 acres of Land, in Hyde county, patented in the name of John HALL, which have not been entered on the list of taxable property, situate in the great pocosin; the said land will be sold..so much thereof as will pay the taxes, &c. the sale..on 5th of August next, at the court-house in German-town. At the same time and place will be sold, or as much of 8000 acres of Land in Hyde county, situate near the head of Pungo river, as will pay the taxes for..1795 and 1796..supposed to belong to COLLINS, ALLEN and Co.. At the same time and place.. 5000 acres..pay the taxes..for..1796, situate in Hyde county, as the property of Joseph LEECH, Of Newbern. As much of 300 acres.. pay taxes..for..1795 and 1796, as the property of John SMITH. At the same time..640 acres of Land, situate at the head of Pungo river..or as much as will pay the taxes for two years, and other charges by Thomas JONES. At the same time..25 acres..near the Lodgham's, formerly belonging to Jesse CANNON, for to pay its taxes two years. At the same time..500 acres pay taxes now due..on Pungo river..property of David JONES. At the same time..100 acres..in Currituck, as the property of Joshua LACY..taxes due thereon. At the same time..640 acres..taxes due..as the property of the late William PALMER, &c. Ephraim ELSBRE, Sheriff. Hyde county, May 15, 1797.

Vol. XII. THURSDAY, June 15, 1797. Numb. 595.

(395) Norfolk, June 8. A Philadelphia paper of the 1st instant, contains the following nominations by the President of the United States: General Charles Cotesworth PINCKNEY, of South Carolina. Francis DANA, Chief Justice of the state of Massachusetts, and General John MARSHAL of Virginia, to be jointly and severally, envoys extra ordinary and Ministers Plenipotentiary to the French Republic. The Senate have confirmed the nomination of John Q. ADAMS, as Minister to the court of Berlin, 17 to 12.

(396) Notice. That on the 5th of August next, at the court house in Germantown, for cash, will be sold, several tracts or parcels of Land in Hyde county, or as much as will pay the taxes due thereon, to wit, 2,464 acres, situate on Broad creek, Pantigo, Swan-quarter,

(396) (Cont.) Piney grove, and Winfield creeks, as the property of John ALLEN; 30,000 acres situate on Juniper bay and Pungo river, or near them and the great Pocosin; and a half acre lot, as the property of John ALEXANDER, in the town of Woodstock; and a half acre lot in said town, as the property of Peter LUSHLEY. Ephraim ELSBRE, Sheriff.

(397) State of North-Carolina. Chowan county, June 8, 1797. Notice is hereby given to all the creditors of Thomas MING, of the said county..is dead, and that the subscriber qualified as administratrix to the estate of the said deceased, in last June term... Delilah MING, Adm'x.

Vol. XII. THURSDAY, June 22, 1797. Numb. 596.

(398) New-York, June 5. Thomas PAINE was to have taken passage to America in the Dublin Packet, from Havre-de-Grace, but the Captain refused to take him. We presume the owner will applaud the Captain's conduct; as PAINE would certainly come to a bad market.

(399) June 9. Capt. Charles WHITE, late of the brig Trio, which was condemned at the Havanna, arrived yesterday from the above place, in the brig Flora.

(400) Baltimore, June 7. The ship Sidney, of this port, Capt. James PARKER (?), from Surinam to Baltimore, was captured on the 12th of April, by a British privateer, the Portland of Antigua and sent into St. KITT's...

(401) The Commissioners for carrying into effect the sixth article of the treaty of Amity, Commerce and Navigation, concluded between his Brittanic Majesty and the United States of America, on the 19th day of November, 1794,..do hereby give notice that they are ready to proceed to business accordingly.. By order of the Board, Griffith EVANS, Secretary. Philadelphia, Commissioners Office, No. 3, South-Sixth street, May 29, 1797.

(402) Edenton, June 16, 1797. Mr. Lewis BERNARD, Sir, Whereas in consideration of monies by me laid out and expended, I sued out an attachment against two half acre lots,...situate in the town of Edenton, and in the new plan of said town distinguished by the numbers 124, and 125, (said to be your property) which attachment was returned to the last term of the court of pleas and quarter sessions for the county of Chowan..at next term of said court, the said property will be exposed to sale..unless you will then appear and shew cause..why said sale should not take place, pursuant to an order of the said court. Honorie NIEL.

(403) State of North-Carolina. Hertford county, June 20, 1797. Notice is hereby given, to all whom it may concern, that John YOUNG, of the county aforesaid, is dead, and that the subscriber qualified as administrator to his estate in November last... James JONES, Adm.

(404) Petersburg, June 6. A man by the name of John CONNER who had resided in Richmond..having been in the habit of forging powers of attorney to draw the arrears of pay due to soldiers in Georgia ..and near 1500 dollars paid before the fraud was discovered.. John CONNER, who it is said came from Georgia, Committed for further trial.

(405) On Tuesday last, commenced the races at New Market-The first day's purse of 100 l. was won by Mr. Samuel TYLER's horse, Chanticleer-the second days purse of 100 dollars by Mr. Daniel WILSON's horse Blazing Star-the third, a sweepstake of 125 guineas, was won by Mr. John VERELL's horse Milo-and on the fourth day, the New Market Silver Cup was won by Mr. Isaac ALLEN's mare Slow and Easy.

Supplement. Vol. XII. THURSDAY, June 22, 1797. Numb. 596.

Vol. XII. THURSDAY, June 29, 1797. Numb. 597.

(406) Savannah, June 2. Arrived on Tuesday last, sloop Larker Captain Robt. LIGHTBURN from New-Providence.. Yesterday arrived the schooner New-Adventure, Captain Samuel S. LIGHTBURN, 4 days from New-Providence...

(407) Edenton, June 29. The subscriber informs the public, that he has just received from New-York, and is now opening, at the store of Mr. F. LITTLE, opposite Mr. O'MALLEY's tavern, a large.. assortment of genuine Drugs and Medicines.. Electricity having been found highly useful in..rheumatisms, lameness, deafness and defect of light, all persons who may be desirous of experiencing its good effects, will please apply to the subscriber, who has a warranted machine, with an insolating stool and medical apparatus complete. John CUNNINGHAM. Edenton, June 25, 1797.

(408) Odd Volumes. A Number of Books in the library of the deceased William CUMMING, being missing, those persons who are in possession..please send them to the subscriber. The property of William CUMMING, deceased, will be sold, at the house of Col. John HAMILTON, near Edenton, on the 21st of July next... James HATHAWAY, Adm.

(409) Notice. To be sold at Benjamin HARDISON's, in Plymouth, on Saturday the second day of September next, if the taxes are not paid before, 100,000 acres of Land, lying in the county of Tyrell, on the east side of Alligator river, or as much as will pay the taxes..for..1796; said land was granted to John G. BLOUNT, and is now supposed to be owned by Robert MORRIS, of the city of Philadelphia. Given under my hand, at Tyrrell, this 20th June, 1797. E. BLOUNT, Sheriff.

(410) To be Sold, on Saturday, the 22d of next month, at Plymouth, The Schooner Betsey and Nancy, of Skewarkey, about 90 tons burthen, nearly new..rigging, sails, &c. belonging to the estate of John BENNETT, dec... Amey BENNETT, Adm'x. Hogston, June 26th, 1797.

Vol. XII. THURSDAY, July 6, 1797. Numb. 598.

(411) New-York, June 16. Naire SMITH, Pardon SMITH, Samuel SPRING, and Richard GRAHAM, were convicted in the Circuit Court of the United States now sitting in Boston, for counterfeiting and passing bank bills of the United States.

(412) Norfolk, June 26. Extract from a letter, dated Philadelphia, June 14. "Last week was a terrible time here among the fighting folks. Mr. BLOUNT was angry at Mr. THATCHER for something he said in Congress; and..Mr. BLOUNT sent him a challenge, which Mr. THATCHER refused to accept; then Mr. Benjamin BLODGET, a Bostonian, came publicly forward, and offered to fight Mr. BLOUNT-so the matter rests."

(413) Appointments. The President of the United States has nominated Elbridge GERRY, Esq. of Massachusetts, Envoy Extraordinary and Minister Plenipotentiary to the French Republic, in the place of Fran__s DANA, Esq. who has declined the appointment.

(414) Edenton, July 6. Notice. Whereas I bought a parcel of land..of John Lewis Baptist MOIGNARD, of Beaufort county, said to contain 470 acres, for which Josiah RASOR and myself gave said MOIGNARD 3 notes of hand, to the amount of 470 pounds, one of which is partly paid off; and after having the land run out, I find but 110 acres of the same, which is a fraud of 360 pounds, ..forwarn..from buying or trading for the..notes, as he has been requested to refund them back to me. Thomas ASHBURN. Bertie, June 29, 1797.

(415) To Be Let. Till the first of January..house, at present occupied by the subscriber..on the 11th will be sold some genteel furniture and kitchen utensils... Bab. M'LAINE. Edenton, July 5, 1797.

Vol. XII. THURSDAY, July 13, 1797. Numb. 599.

(416) Edenton, July 13. Extract of a letter from Londonderry, April 16. "Ireland still continues in a convulsed and critical situation; God only knows when it will end."

(417) Notice. That on the 27th of August next, for cash, will be sold, at the court-house in Germantown, Hyde county,..parcels of land which have not been enlisted for taxation agreeable to law: Fifty acres, as the property of Francis WARD..in Tarkiln neck, and on Wright's creek. 400 acres in New Currituck, joining James CLEAVE's land, as the property of Mary SILVESTER. 300 acres in Tarkiln neck, on the North Dividing creeks, as the property of Jas. ALDERSON's heirs. 150 acres on Jordan's creek, as the property of Thomas ELLERSON, dec. 500 acres on Mattamuskeet, near Furr (?) creek, as the property of Willis WILSON, of Virginia. 100 acres on the Beach Ridge, joining George DAVENPORT's land, as the property of Joel DAVENPORT. 190 acres on the head of Sinclar's creek, as the property of Wm. PRICE, of Beaufort. 640 acres as the property of Hosea MORTON, on the head of Pungo river. 200 acres on the head of Pungo river, as the property of James JONES. 200 acres on the head of said river, joining his former land. 100 acres on

(417) (Cont.) or near the head of Pungo river, as the property of Thomas BEDFORD. 100 acres on the southermost end of Ray's ridge, as the property of John BRIGHT. 50 acres joining ___ SMITH's line, as the property of John BRIGHT. 100 a. in the Indian Run swamp, as the property of Thomas ROGERS, of Bath. 16,500 acres in the pocosin between Mattamuskeet and Currituck, and on or near Broad creek. 640 do. do. 50 acres in the lake at the mouth of the Canal, as the property of Vallentine NIHELL. 6400 acres HANCOCK's and TODDNY's line, on Swan-Quarter, as the property of Thomas PARKER. 8000 acres lying on the head of the Indian Run and Pungo rivers, as the property of John LEWIS, senior. 800 acres on Swan-Quarter, as the property of Joseph PIQUETT, joining Josiah JARVIS's line. 300 acres on the head of Long Shoal river, in the Juniper Swamp. 3,200 acres on the east-side of Mattamuskeet lake, joining John HUNT's land, as the property of William SMITH, of Baltimore. 125 acres on Swan-Quarter, joining Josiah JARVIS's land. 100 acres on Jordan creek, as the property of BUSKMAN, in Maryland. Ephraim ELSBRE, Sheriff. July 8th, 1797.

(418) John LITTLE, Has for sale..just received from Liverpool, Salt, Liverpool China and Queens Ware..Stoneware... July 11, 1797.

(419) North-Carolina, Chowan county, ss. June Term, 1797. Henry WARREN, by Attorney, vs. Joseph & Nath W. OTIS, Attachment. Robert MOODY, summoned as garnishee, and garnishment rendered. Default and Enquiry In the above suit, Joseph and Nath. W. OTIS, being alledged as merchants of the city of Charleston, in South-Carolina, it was then ordered by the worshipful the Justices of the said county court, that notice of the above suit be given in the State Gazette for..three weeks... By order, Elisha NORFLEET, C. C. C. C.

(420) On the 24th inst. at Washington, will be sold, at auction.. The Hull of a new Vessel.. Any person desirous to view and examine her, may do so..at the ship-yard of Mr. John RUSSEL, in Hyde, who is the builder. She hath heretofore been known by the name of Harmony Hall. J. ALDERSON. Washington, July 7th, 1797.

(421) Henry KENNEDY, At the head of Capt. BUTLER's wharf,..has just received from New-York, an assortment of Good Leather, with which he can supply their demands in the Boot and Shoe-making line... Edenton, July 11, 1797.

(422) State of North-Carolina. Pasquotank county, July 10, 1797. Notice is hereby given, to all whom it may concern, that William E. WRIGHT, of the county aforesaid, is dead, and that the subscriber qualified as executor to his estate in June last... John LANE, Ex'r.

Vol. XII. THURSDAY, July 20, 1797. Numb. 600.

(423) New-York, June 21. The Secretary of State of the United States has reported to the President on the proceedings of Andrew ELLICOT, Esq. the commissioner for running the boundary line between the United States and the two Floridas.

(424) Philadelphia, July 7. William BLOUNT took his seat in the Senate yesterday, as usual. He read a short address, in which he said he trusted when he came to be heard upon his trial, he should be able to clear himself from the charges..to be brought against him..resolved That the said William BLOUNT, be taken into the custody of the messenger of the House,..until ___ surety for his appearance to the charges..against him..in the sum of 20,000 dollars, and sureties in 15,000 dollars each.. Mr. BLOUNT immediately entered into bond for 20,000 dollars, and Pierce BUTLER, Esq. and Thomas BLOUNT, Esq. each of them in bonds of 15,000 dollars as his sureties.

(425) Edenton, July 20. Died, at Eden-House, on Monday morning last, Mrs. Penelope DAWSON.

(426) Letters remaining in the Post-Office at Edenton, July 1st, 1797. Benjamin ATKINSON, Nicholas ATKINS, Daniel BRADLEY, John BLOUNT, Capt. James ARCHIBALD, William BLOUNT, Arthur BROWN, James Henry BROWN, Gen. Lawrence BAKER, James BAKER, John BROWN, James CARMER, Mrs. Margaret CARRUTHERS, Samuel COVERLY, jun., Isaac CLARK, 2, Colin CAMPBELL, Nathaniel DOWNS, Capt. Jonathan DUBOIS, John D. DAVIS, Hayden EDGAR, James FRAME, Capt. Thomas GARRET, John GOELET, Jas. HOLMES, Mary GILELAND, David HAUGHTON, Hugh CUMMING, Capt. Elisha JONES, Mrs. Betsey LANG, Joseph LILLIBRIDGE, Capt. B. LEE, Patrick M'ARTHUR, Solomon James M'CANNA, Charles MOORE, Samuel MAIR, Nathaniel NICKERSON, Capt. John NORCOM, John NORCOM (sic), Gilbert M'INTYRE, Charles PETTIGREW, Doctor Elisha PERKINS, Doctor John D. PERKINS, Capt. Herbert PRIDE, Benjamin POYNER, Z. Currey PRESCOT, Rev. Martin ROSS, Mrs. RONDET, John RAVENS, Dr. Peyton ROSE, Thomas RYAN, Malachi SAWYER, Enoch SAWYER, Sheriff of Tyrrell county, Benjamin SPRUILL, William SMITH, Elizabeth STEELE, David SAWYER, Sheriff of Gates county, Capt. Theophilus STETSON, Robert SMITH, Emos SMITH, Benjamin TAYLOR, Kinchen TURNER, William THOMSON, Thomas TROTTER, Elisha WILLIAMS, Capt. Thomas WHITE, William WHEATON, Zatthu M. WHITALL, Henry WARRICK, Thomas WILLIAMS, Thomas VAIL. Hend. STANDIN, P. M.

(427) Grand Lodge. The Officers and Members of the Grand Lodge ..are hereby requested to attend the annual communication in the city of Raleigh, on the evening of Thursday, the 30th November next, at 6 o'clock. By order of the Most Worshipful William R. DAVIE, Grand Master. Robert WILLIAMS, jun. Grand Secretary.

(428) Twenty Dollars Reward. Run away, on the 7th of May, 1796 (sic), a Lad, of about 17 or 18 years of age..return him to me in Currituck county... Jesse SIMMONS.

Vol. XII. THURSDAY, July 27, 1797. Numb. 601.

(429) Norfolk, July 19. Appointments By Authority. William SMITH, of South Carolina, Minister Plenipotentiary to Portugal-Vice John Q. ADAMS, removed to Berlin. Thomas BULKLEY (?), Consul at Portugal. Richard O'BRIEN, Consul General with the Dey and Regency of Algiers. Charles HALL, of Pennsylvania, Agent of the United States ..in relation to the 6th article of the treaty with Great Britain.

(429) (Cont.) Jeremiah SMITH, of New Hampshire, Attorney of that district, in the room of Edward St. Lue (?) LIVERMORE, resigned. William WILLIS, Consul with the Republic of Venice. Frederick H. WALLASTON, Consul of the United States, in the Republic of Genoa-Vice F. CHILDS, resigned. James L_nder CATHCART, Consul within the city and kingdom of Tripoli. William EATON, Consul within the city and kingdom of Tunis. William HORT (?), Naval Officer of the district of South Carolina.

(430) Portsmouth, July 1. Frigate of the United States! On Thursday last a beautiful copper bottomed frigate pierced for 36 guns was launched from the navy yard.. Said ship was built by Col. James HACKET..and is supposed to be designed as a present for..the Dey of Algiers. Capt. Thomas THOMPSON, of Portsmouth, superintendant for building and equipping the frigate for sea.. Josiah FOX, of Philadelphia, navy constructor, draughted and moulded the frigate...

(431) New-York, July 12. We are assured that Capt. Nathan HALEY, who was said to be taken in the ship Hare, was himself the man who conducted her into France.

(432) Philadelphia, July 10. In the Senate, on Saturday morning, the order of the day was called for on the motion for expelling William BLOUNT from his seat in the Senate.. July 11. The Senate notified the house of the measures they had taken in respect to Mr. William BLOUNT, a late Senator, in regard to the conspiracy he had engaged in with the British to invade the Spanish territory, not as the British Minister had disavowed, of Louisiana, but of the adjacent country of the Floridas...

(433) July 13. The following facts, relative to the capture of the ship Nancy, belonging to Mr. William DAVY of this city, are well worthy the attention of our merchants...

(434) Edenton, July 27. Married, on the 4th inst. at the house of Mr. Michael FENNELL, in Camden county, Mr. Charles GRICE, to Miss Peggy JONES, daughter of Joseph JONES, Esq. And on Tuesday last, at Mr. Joshua SKINNER's, in Perquimans, Mr. Willoughby DAUGE, to Miss Polly SUMNER.

Vol. XII. THURSDAY, August 3, 1797. Numb. 602.

(435) New-York, July 19. The tribunal of commerce in Havre-de-Grace have declared the capture of the ship Juliana, Captain Thomas HOWARD, to be Null and Illegal. The Juliana was bound from Baltimore to Bremen.

(436) Edenton, August 3. Whereas my wife Margaret JONES has absconded from my bed and board, without any just cause, I do..forwarn all persons..from crediting..her on my account... James JONES. July 27th, 1797.

(437) (From a New York paper.) Two Remarkable Facts. On the 14th of April last, Mr. Allen TAYLOR, grocer of this city, purchased a

(437) (Cont.) cask of hog's lard, weighing about 212 lbs. which he continued selling by retail until about the 12th of May, when at the bottom was found inclosed in the fat, a living Hen, supposed to have continued thus imprisoned ever since last fall, the lard having been in possession of Mr. James CARTER about a month before it was sold to Mr. TAYLOR..she is now alive and in good condition.. Mr. Allen TAYLOR, No. 59 Barclay street..can vouch for the fact...

On Tuesday fe'night, Mr. Nathaniel WHITMORE was struck by lightening at the ferry opposite Shenectady.. As his coat, shirt, and overalls were rent by the lightening in many places, his boots torn from his legs, and two dollars in his waistcoat pocket perforated, his recovery may be considered very providential.

Vol. XII. THURSDAY, August 10, 1797. Numb. 603.

(438) Edenton, August 10. Notice. Being called upon by the heirs of Peter NOUGIER, deceased, for the settlement of his estate. .. William BORRITZ, Adm. Edenton, August 2d, 1797.

(439) Taken up and committed to the gaol of this town, a negro wench named RHODY, who says she belongs to Benjamin SPURR, of Charleston, South-Carolina. She is about 30 years of age, 5 feet 8 or 10 inches high, pretty thick set.. She says she has a husband with her named ISRAEL, who is supposed to be lurking about there... Zachariah WEBB, Gaoler. Edenton, August 8th, 1797.

(440) Boston, July 10. Extract of a letter written by Capt. W. S. PLUMMER, of the brig Telemachus, to R. MONTGOMERY, Esq. American Consul at Alicant, dated Carthagena, May 20... Wm. S. PLUMMER (To) Robert MONTGOMERY, Esq.

Vol. XII. THURSDAY, August 17, 1797. Numb. 604.

(441) Edenton, August 17. The following returns have come to hand of the late election. Chowan-Lemuel CREECY, senate. Richard BENBURY and Benjamin COFFIELD, commons. Thomas JOHNSON, for the town of Edenton. Perquimans-Senator not certainly known from a mistake in giving the votes. Candidates, Joseph HARVEY and Francis NEWBY. John SKINNER and Joseph WHITE, commons. Bertie-Francis PUGH, senate. George OUTLAW and James B. JORDAN, commons. Pasquotank-Thomas BANKS, senate. William FARANGE and Bailey JACKSON, commons. Camden- ____ TORKSEY, senate. Enoch DALEY and Zephaniah BURGES, commons. Currituck- ____ PHILIPS, senate. Beaufort-Hans PATTEN, senate. Thomas ELLISON and Frederick GRICE, commons.

(442) The situation of my affairs being such as to require an immediate settlement of my accounts, I do..in the most pressing manner, solicit all those indebted to me, indiscriminately, to call and settle their respective accounts... Henry WILLS. Edenton, August 12, 1797.

(443) The subscriber has for sale, at his store No. 7, on Cheapside, the best Manufactured Tobacco, in legs and small twists... R. A. SQUIRES. Edenton, August 12, 1797.

(444) University of North-Carolina, July 18, 1797. An examination of the Students commenced under the direction of Mr. CALDWELL and Mr. HOLMES, Professors; and Mr. LELVAUX and Mr. RICHARDS, Tutors in the preparatory school, on the 14th of July, and ended the 18th. The undersigned Trustees attended...John WILLIAMS, James HOGG, Adlai OSBORNE, Benj. WILLIAMS, Walter ALVES, Willie JONES.

Vol. XII. THURSDAY, August 24, 1797. Numb. 605.

(445) Romayne's Letter. To the Editors of the New-York Gazette and General Advertiser..Mr. Richard HARRISON, the Attorney of New York, who seems foolishly active in Mr. BLOUNT's prosecution... N. ROMAYNE. New York, July 27, 1797.

(446) Edenton, August 24. Further returns of Members of Assembly, chosen at the late elections. Craven-Wm. M'CLURE, senate. Wm. BLACKLEDGE and Henry TILLMAN, commons. For the town of Newbern-Edward GRAHAM. Halifax-Colonel Stephen CARNEY, senate. Col. James TABB and Wood J. HAMLIN, commons. Halifax town-Thaddeus BARNES. Northampton-John BINFORD, senate. Benjamin WILLIAMSON and Nicholas EDMUNDS, commons. Nash-Archibald GRIFFIN, senate. Archibald HUNTER and Redmund BUNN (?), commons.

(447) Died, in Pasquotank, on the 6th inst. Enoch RELFE, Esq. Clerk of the county court of that county.

(448) Thomas B. LITTLEJOHN and Co. Have for Sale, Jamaica and Winward Island Rum..Sugar..Coffee..Molasses..Sherry Wine..Bar-Iron. August 22, 1797.

(449) For Sale, Rosin, and Spirits of Turpentine... Robert MOODY.

(450) Dry Goods. The subscriber being about to leave this state.. has consigned his Goods to Mr. Jeremiah GALLOP, to be sold on commission... Peter MAXTON. Edenton, Aug. 17, 1797.

(451) 15 Dollars Reward. Run Away from the subscriber, on the 12th of April, 1797, a young negro fellow named FRANK, about 23 years of age, 5 feet 4 inches high, well set, thick lips, and stutters in his speech, formerly belonging to Richard BENBURY... Benjamin MANNING. Edgcomb county, Aug. 20, 1797.

(452) Run Away from the subscriber, on the 16th instant, a negro fellow named HARRY, about 5 feet 10 or 11 inches high, of a yellowish complexion, very thick set, and has an out-mouth... Wm. JACKSON. August 23, 1797.

Vol. XII. THURSDAY, August 31, 1797. Numb. 606.

(453) Petersburg, August 25. An alarm having prevailed in Philadelphia respecting the appearance of the Yellow Fever..the Gov. of Pennsylvania wrote, on the 14th inst. to the College of Physicians of Philadelphia..Dr. John REDMAN, President of the College, returned for answer on the 16th, that it was evident that a malignant contagious fever, has lately appeared in Penn-street and its vicinity.

(454) Edenton, August 31. We are authorized to inform the public that Major Joseph HARVEY has been elected senator for the county of Perquimans. Further returns of Members of Assembly chosen at the late election. <u>Gates</u>-Joseph RIDDICK, senate. Jas. GATLING and ____ HUTCHINGS, commons. <u>Tyrrell</u>-Charles SPRUILL, senate. John GUITHER and James HOSKINS, commons. <u>Hertford</u>-Thos. WYNNS, senate. Robert MONTGOMERY and Jas. JONES, commons. <u>Pitt</u>-Samuel SIMPSON, senate. Holland JOHNSTON and Wm. GRIMES, commons. <u>Edgcomb</u>-Col. Nathan MAYO, senate. Frederick PHILLIPS and Mr. GILBERT, commons. <u>Martin</u>-Wm. M'KINZIE, senate. Jeremiah SLADE and John HYMAN, commons. <u>Franklin</u>-Henry HILL, senate. Britain HARRIS and John FOSTER, commons. <u>Nash</u>-Archibald GRIFFIN, senate. Archibald HUNTER and E. BUNN, commons. <u>Hyde</u>-Henry SILBY, senate. Simon ALDERSON and J. WATSON, commons. <u>Jones</u>-John HATCH, senate. Amos JOHNSON and William BASH, commons. <u>New-Hanover</u>-John HILL, senate. Samuel ASHE and Duncan MOORE, commons. <u>Wilmington</u>-Wm. H. HILL, <u>Onslow</u>-Christopher DUDLEY, senate. Joseph S. CRAY and Nathaniel LOOMISS, commons.

(455) Died, on Thursday last, at the house of Capt. S. BUTLER, Miss Anne JONES, daughter of the late Thomas JONES, Esq. of this town.

(456) North-Carolina. Treasury Office, Aug. 10, 1797. On the sixth day of October next commences the Superior Court for the district of Hillsborough:-On that day it will become the..duty of the Public Treasurer to proceed against all persons..then in arrears to the state... John HAYWOOD, Public Treasurer.

(457) To be Let until the 1st of January next, The Part of the House adjoining the Printing-Office, lately occupied by Capt. Daniel YOUNG. For terms apply to the Printer.

Vol. XII. THURSDAY, September 7, 1797. Numb. 607.

(458) From the <u>Merchant's Advertiser</u>. (Letter to) Mr. BRADFORD (from) John Allen FINCH...

(459) Baltimore, August 22. Alexandria, Aug. 18, 1797. (Letter) John TOWERS, Master of the ship Saratoga (To) Messrs. YUNDT and BROWN...

Vol. XII. THURSDAY, September 14, 1797. Numb. 608.

(460) Halifax, September 4. Agreeably to a notice of his Excellency the Governor, the Council of State convened at the city of Raleigh, on Tuesday the 29th of August last; when was nominated and appointed the Hon. Major General Thomas BROWN, President, and Robert WILLIAMS, jun., Secretary.

Vol. XII. THURSDAY, September 21, 1797. Numb. 609.

(461) Mr. WILLS. Many doubts having arisen respecting the election of a Senator for the county of Perquimans, and being censured for my conduct on the occasion; I think it necessary to lay before

(461) (Cont.) the public a true statement of the business...
Edward HALL, Sheriff of Perquimans county.

(462) Baltimore, Sept. 1. For these two evenings past the Comet which was seen to the eastward, has been observed here, on his way to the sun. His direction last evening appeared to the eye about E.S.E..

(463) Edenton, September 21. Friday last arrived the schooner Little Gabriel, Leven BOZMAN, master, from Antigua.

(464) A Meeting of the Commissioners for repairing the Court-House is requested at the town of Edenton, on the 13th of October next, in order to receive the Court-House, and finally settle their accounts. This meeting is earnestly wished to take place punctually, in order to obviate the difficulties in settling the estate of the deceased William LEWIS, which further delays would occasion. Joseph RIDDICK. Sept. 13th, 1797.

(465) State of North-Carolina. Pasquotank county, Sept. 18, 1797. Notice is hereby given, to all whom it may concern, that Enoch RELFE, Esq. of the county aforesaid, is dead, and that the subscriber qualified as administrator to his estate in the last term... William T. MUSE, Adm.

Vol. XII. THURSDAY, September 28, 1797. Numb. 610.

(466) Edenton, September 28. Land Negroes and Cattle. For Sale. A Very valuable Tract of Land, containing 250 acres, at present possessed by Mr. DE CLUGNEY, within three miles of Edenton; on the premises there is a very comfortable mansion house, and out-houses suitable for a plantation... John HAMILTON. Near Edenton, Sept. 22, 1797.

(467) Proclamation. Whereas I have received information that a certain Ezekiel POLK, John JOHNSTON, and others, of Mecklenburg county in this state..set on foot and prepare for carrying on, a military expedition for the invasion of and taking..the territory of the Indians, on the Tennessee, with whom the United States are at peace..I do..issue this Proclamation, strictly charging..all officers of Justice, and others, to apprehend and secure and bring to justice, the said Ezekiel POLK, John JOHNSTON, and other principal delinquents, if to be found in this state... Given under my hand and seal at arms, at Raleigh, the first day of September, A. D. 1797, and in the XXII year of American Independence. Samuel ASHE. By command, Roger MOORE, Private Sec'ry.

Vol. XII. THURSDAY, October 5, 1797. Numb. 611.

(468) Alexandria, Sept. 25. In the *Times* of Saturday, August 9, was the following paragraph: "The following was handed us for publication by a gentleman lately from Guadaloupe. That one John PERRY, lately of New-London, and a certain Park AVERY are equally concerned in fitting out privateers from several French ports in the West-Indies, to cruise for American property, and that the

(468) (Cont.) plunder they have obtained was shipped to the house of Elisha and William COIT, of New-York. Isaac WILLIAMS, who is also an American, is captain of one of their privateers, and had captured several Americans." On Saturday last the person of PERRY was recognized on the wharf.. By the depositions of Captain WILLIS and Mr. Peter MURRAY, it was evident that his vessel, immediately upon her arrival in Guadaloupe, was converted into a privateer, and called the Victorious, and was commanded by an American of the name of WILLIAMS... He was committed to prison for further examination.

(469) Norfolk, Sept. 30. Capt. Timothy NEWMAN is appointed to the command of the Crescent frigate, at Portsmouth, New-Hampshire, designed for the Dey of Algiers.

(470) Edenton, October 5. Letters remaining in the Post-Office at Edenton, October 1st, 1797. Captain James ARCHIBALD, Capt. Joseph BRYAN, Hezekiah BROADWELL, Arthur BROWN, Gen. Lawrence BAKER, Thomas West BRIMAGE, Esq., Col. William BAKER, Dr. John CHAMBERLAN, Capt. Douglas CHAPMAN, Capt. James DUNSCOMB, Monsieur DE NARD, Monsieur DE CLUGNEY, Mrs. Venice EVANS, Hugh FINCH, Mrs. Eliza GOELET, George GORDON, James GREGORY, James GILLESPIE, Esq., Mr. JOHERES, Seth LANDS, Capt. Daniel LATHARE, Ens. Niel M'ALPINE, Bab. M'LAINE, Archibald M'LEOD, Miss Hushin MIELES, Donald M'INTYRE, John NICHOLLS, Ann B. POLLOK, Mess. BOARDMAN & SEYMOUR, Rebecca SWANN, Madame DE SERCEY, Batis DAL VACHO, Thomas WARRENTON, Abner WHITING, Samuel WHITING, Captain Thomas WHITE, Malachi WOLSEY, Executors or Administrators of William J. DAWSON. Henderson STANDIN, P. M.

(471) Notice. Being now confined in the public gaol of Edenton, on an execution at the instance of Honorie NIEL, merchant in Edenton..I intend on the 18th day of October next..to take the benefit of the insolvent law of this state. Henry WARRICK. Edenton gaol, Sept. 28, 1797.

Vol. XII. THURSDAY, October 12, 1797. Numb. 612.

(472) Philadelphia, Sept. 25. The brig Betsey, Capt. ART,..was, on Sunday last, captured by a French privateer within 3 miles of the Capes of Delaware. Vessel and cargo were the property of Mess. Thomas HARRISON, John EVANS and John COX.

(473) Savannah, Sept. 15. On the 12th inst. arrived at Cockspur, the schooner Exuma, Captain Daniel CALLAGHAN, from New-Providence. The 9th inst. in lat. 29, 39, long. 79, 42 picked up the long boat of the armed ship General Nichols, Captain Michael MORRISON, belonging to Grenada. The Gen. Nichols, left New-Providence on the 2d inst. with Negroes, supposed for this port, _____vy gale of wind, on the 8th foundered (?). The long boat and yawl, with hardly time to get from her, when she went down with 122 of the cargo. In the long boat were saved 5 whites and __ negroes, and when they got along side the Exuma, had nothing to eat or drink. The yawl (having sails) with the Capt. and Peter MORRIS, supercargo, five other ____ and three negroes, parted company with the

(473) (Cont.) other boat, immediately after leaving the ship, and has not yet been heard of.

(474) Savannah, Sept. 19. On Sunday last, arrived in port, the schooner Nancy, of Philadelphia, John BURNETT, master..in lat. 24, 40, long. 81, ___, he was chased and brought too, by a ___ish privateer brig, called the Camp___, commanded by Capt. WILSON, and belonging to New-Providence. On the 12th, Capt. BURNETT,.. with the assistance of his mate, Mr. Samuel (?) CLARK, got posesion of their ___, threw them overboard, and secured the prize-master, and his crew, and brought them safely to this place...

(475) Norfolk, October 5. Died, Lately in Iveraah, Ireland, aged 112, Daniel Bull MACARTHY, Esq.. He was married to five wives; he married the fifth, who survives him, when he was 84, and she 14, by whom he had 20 children, bearing a child every year.

(476) Edenton, October 12. State of North-Carolina. Bertie county, October 8, 1797. Notice is hereby given, to all whom it may concern, that Sarah MEREDITH, of the county aforesaid, is dead, and that the subscribers qualified as administrators to her estate at the last term... Thomas BROWNRIGG, Joseph A. BROWN, Adm's.

Vol. XII. THURSDAY, October 19, 1797. Numb. 613.

(477) Pittsburg, Sept. 23. A few days ago, a white man by name of CLERK, was killed by an Indian on Beaver Creek...

(478) Norfolk, October 11. At a court held lately at Albany, Simeon BRANDT was sentenced for life to imprisonment and hard labour, for passing knowingly, two counterfeit quarter dollars.

(479) Notice. The subscriber having administered on the estate of Francis SPEIGHT, deceased, at the last August court held for the county of Gates... William GOODMAN, Adm. October 11th, 1797.

Vol. XII. THURSDAY, November 2, 1797. Numb. 615.

STATE GAZETTE OF NORTH-CAROLINA.
EDENTON: Printed by James WILLS.

(480) Boston, October 9. Copy of a letter from an American Agent for British Spoiliations. London, August 10, 1797. (From) Samuel CABOT...(To) Mr. John BRAZER.

(481) Portsmouth (N. H.) October 7. Capt. KENNARD, of the brig Brothers, on his passage from Grenada, to Portsmouth, N. H..Sept. 1, was boarded by a small privateer schooner..robbed.. Nathaniel KENNARD, master, Hiram COFFIN, mate, Wm. COLE, seaman, Attested.

(482) Edenton, November 2. Died, on Friday evening last, Mr. Ivey PURDY, a respectable and worthy inhabitant of this town.

(483) H. WILLS, having entirely resigned the Printing Business in Edenton in favour of his brother James WILLS, solicits respectfully

(483) (Cont.) that a continuance of the favours of the public may be conferred on him, so long as they conceive him deserving of them.

(484) James WILLS, being desirous of establishing himself in Edenton, and having complete apparatus for carrying on the printing business, proposes to continue the publication of the State Gazette on the same terms as it has been heretofore conducted... Printing-Office, Edenton, Nov. 2, 1797.

Vol. XIII. THURSDAY, January 18, 1798. Number 626.

(485) New-York, December 25. We have received the following information with respect to the liberation of John UNDERWOOD, Joseph PRESSEY and John MITCHELL, three of our countrymen, from their confinement on board the British sloop of war, the Hunter, Capt. Tudor TUCKER, now lying in this port.. Underwood procured the means of writing..his friends..Captain Jacob CROWNENSHIELD, of Salem, in Massachusetts, a friend..of UNDERWOOD..took immediate measures for the obtainment of his liberation...

(486) Philadelphia, December 29. On Saturday last, the dwelling house of Archibald Hamilton ROWAN, Esq. on Brandywine Creek, together with all the valuable effects contained therein, was totally destroyed by fire.

(487) Richmond, December 19. Married-on the 13th ultimo, by the Rev. Mr. CHASTAIN, Alexander MITCHELL, Esq. aged 109 years, (much afflicted with the palsy) to the amiable and accomplished Miss Jane HAMMOND, aged 16 years-both of Buckingham county.

(488) Norfolk, Jan. 11. Tuesday evening arrived here, in great distress, the sloop Rambler, bound from Washington (N. C.) to Philadelphia; out 50 days, and had been blown off the coast seven times. On the 18th ult. spoke the schooner Nancy, Ben. WILSON, master, from George-Town (S. C.) in lat. 39, long. 68, out 35 days, in very great distress.

(489) Norfolk, Jan. 13. The ship Margaret, of Baltimore, William COWARD, master, arrived in Hampton Roads on the 4th inst. after a passage of 115 days from Bremen, having been on the coast 8 weeks in very severe weather. On the 28th of November, fell in with the wreck of the sloop Industry, of Currituck, John CHURCH appearing by the papers on board to have been master, lat. 35, 20, long. 69 W. no person on board nor boat. Dec. 31 spoke the ship Joseph, of Portland, B. STONE, master, who was so kind as to supply Capt. COWARD with provisions, and the same day spoke brig Amazon of New-York, from Cape Nichola Mole, for New-York, 17 days out, John JONES, master, who also supplied Capt. COWARD.

(490) Edenton, January 19. The following letter was read in the House of Representatives of the United States, on the 27th of December, 1797. The President has thought proper to inform me, that my services as Commissioner of the Revenue are no longer required... Tenche COXE. Walnut-street, Dec. 26.

(491) Notice. The Co-partnership of BIXBY and KEITH, is this day dissolved by mutual consent... KEITH and TISDALE, Joseph BIXBY, Nathan BIXBY. Norfolk, January 4, 1798.

(492) On Tuesday, the 13th of February next, will be Sold...before Mr. Jus. WOOD's Tavern..four Lots of Ground, with the Houses thereon, adjoining Mr. WOOD's in the town of Hertford, the property of Mr. William T. SMITH, of Philadelphia, now occupied by Capt. DUBOIS. January 8th, 1798.

(493) Fifteen Dollars Reward. Run away from the Subscriber, in Edenton, on the 16th ult., a Negro Man named ISAAC, about 33 years old, stout made, broad face and a little yellowish.. He can work a little at the shoe making business and has been a voyage or two to sea... Elisha NORFLEET. Edenton, January 16th, 1798.

(494) Just come to hand from New-York, and will be opened in a few days, opposite the Market..Dry Goods, Crockery, Glass and Hard-Ware... J. B. WILLIAMS. January 1st, 1798.

(495) To Be Rented, For one year..The Store and Ware-House, at present occupied by James FISK... N. ALLEN. Edenton, Jan. 2d, 1798.

(496) Thomas B. LITTLEJOHN and Co. Have for Sale, Jamaica Rum, 2 years old, Coffee, Molasses... November 22d, 1797.

(497) Lands for Sale. On the 28th day of February, 1798, will be Sold, for the taxes due thereon, for the year 1796, at the Court-House in Beaufort, Carteret county..46,720 acres of Land, situated on the head-waters of New-Port river, and on Coor and Bogue Sounds; which..is given in as the property of David ALLISON, by Richard BLACKLEDGE, as his agent. Wm. THOMSON, Jun. Sheriff. November 29th, 1797.

(498) Lands for Sale. On Tuesday, the 30th of January, 1798, will be Sold, for cash, at the Court-House in Onslow county.. 210,260 acres of Land, situated on various branches and head waters of New-river in said county. Some part of which land joins the county lines of New-Hanover, Duplin and Jones. Said land was given in by Richard BLACKLEDGE, as agent for David ALLISON, and to be sold to satisfy the taxes thereon for..1796. Lemuel DOTY, Sheriff. November 28, 1797.

(499) Medicines, Genuine and unadulterated, may be had at the store of Charles W. JANSON, opposite the Court-House, Edenton... January 10, 1798.

(500) Letters remaining in the Post-Office at Edenton, January 1, 1798.- Reuben ARNOLD, 2, Samuel M'ALLISTER, General BAKER, Rynolds BROWN, Col. William BAKER, Richard BENBURY, 2, Henry BAKER, Wm. BATEMAN, Wm. BARTOLL, Jeremiah BARTON, James CARMER, Hugh CAVAUGH, Rev. Edward CONN, Wm. CHURCH, Mr. DAVOZAC, Samuel GRIFFITH, Thomas GORDON, James S. GROVER, Ebenezer GRAHAM, T. HINCHIZ, John HALSEY, John GOELET, Timothy HUNTER, Thomas HANKINS, Sarah HOLLAND, John

(500) (Cont.) M'LACHLAN, Hugh MITHOLAND, James MOORE, Thomas M'COY, Daughald M'MILLAN, Elisha NORFLEET, Rev. Charles PETTIGREW, E. RODNEY, John ROSS, Wm. SPILLER, Mrs. R. SWAN, Wm. SUTTON, Sarah SHINGSTON, Joseph SHEPHERD, The Sheriffs of Gates, Chowan and Tyrrell county, John TUCK, Timothy WALTON, Capt. Thomas WHITE, Samuel WHITING, Messrs. WIGGINS and BON. Hend. STANDIN, P. M.

(501) Notice. Agreeable to the act of Assembly..notice is hereby given that at the house of Mrs. RIPLY, near Elizabeth-Town, in the county of Pasquotank, on the 5th day of February next..sale, to pay the taxes due..Land, called the Great Desart..in Pasquotank county, containing 27,000 acres, as the property of John M'KINNIE, of Orange county, Virginia; and 5000 acres..on the borders of said Desart, in the new lands, as the property of said M'KINNIE... Robert M'MORINE, Sheriff of Pasquotank. Nixonton, Dec. 8, 1797.

(502) Notice. I Do hereby forwarn all persons from trading with Margaret JONES, or boarding, or having any dealings with her or buying any thing from her, as I will not pay any debts of her contracting, or be answerable for her conduct from this date. James JONES. January 1st, 1798.

Vol. XIII. THURSDAY, February 1, 1798. Number 628.

(503) Edenton, February 1. Proclamation. Whereas..last night, the room in the State-house..called the Comptroller's office, was broken into by three villains, and a trunk said to be the property of Wm. TYRREL..which said trunk and papers had been seized..and deposited..for the inspection of the Board of Enquiry;..supposed to contain evidence of the frauds and forgeries lately committed in obtaining military land warrants and grants. At the same time was thrown out of the window..a large chest of James GLASGOW, Esq. filled with papers appertaining to the Secretary of States office, &c... A Reward of Fifty Pounds currency.. Given under my hand and seal at arms, at Raleigh, the 19th day of jan (sic) A. D. 1798. Samuel ASHE. By command, Roger MOORE, Priv. Sec'ry.

(504) Died, on Thursday last, William SKINNER, Esq. Commissioner of Loans for the state of North-Carolina.

(505) Notice. The Subscriber begs leave to inform the public in general..that he continues to keep the Ferry from Mackey's to Edenton, as usual, and has just opened a House of Entertainment, where he now lives, near said Ferry... Myles HARDY. January 27th, 1798.

(506) The High Bred Imported Horse Silver, Much celebrated for his running in England, late the property of Lord SACKVILLE..Was imported from London, in..November last, by John DREW, sen... The above horse will stand the ensuing season at Scotland-Neck, 25 miles below Halifax town, (N. C.) John DREW, jun. Jan. 10.

(507) Philip LARUS, Surgeon and Dentist..lately arrived from Philadelphia..please apply at Mr. Thomas COX's Tavern-Mr. L. will stay but two weeks in Town. Edenton, February 1, 1798.

(508) Proposals For Carrying The Public Mails on the following Post-Roads will be received at the General Post-Office until the 14th day of February next inclusive... Joseph HABERSHAM, Post-Master General. General Post Office, Philadelphia, December 16, 1797.

(509) Hezekia BROADWELL, I Give you this notice, that I have attached James CARMER's Note to you, with other papers in the hands of James HATHAWAY, and shall take judgment the next quarterly court held for the county of Chowan. Humphrey HARDY.

Vol. XIII. THURSDAY, March 1, 1798. Number 632.

(510) Boston, Feb. 5. Consummate villany and murder. (The following very extraordinary letter was handed us on Saturday evening for publication.) States of America, Jan. 1798. Madam, I am one of those people who subsist on the spoils of the traveller, but if the spark of humanity was entirely extinguished from my breast, you would never gain this, or any other information of a person who was very dear to you-You must know madam, that it was my fortune, with two or three of my associates to fall in with Mr. Oliver JOHNSON; after taking from him his cash,..about 1800 dollars, we mutually agreed for our own security to dispatch the said Oliver JOHNSON, and informed him of our determination. Immediately when he saw his fate determined upon he craved these two favours-viz. that we would write to his family which he said lived in Westmoreland, and direct the letter to be left at the Post-Office in Walpole, (N. H.) to inform you of his fate; and his last request is that Col. Joseph BURT, and Ezra PEIRCE, administer upon his estate, and wishes them to assist his distressed family. To the wife of Oliver JOHNSON, late of Westmoreland. A true copy-attest Thomas K. GREEN, Job F. BOOKS, Joseph BURT, J. BUFFUM, Select men of Westmoreland.

(511) Boston, Feb. 14. Yesterday arrived the brig Joseph, Captain HOPKINS, in 28 days from Malaga. Same day, Ship Polly, JONES from Bencoolen, from whence he sailed September 8. On the passage to the Cape of Good-Hope Captain DELANE, who went out master of the ship, died, and was committed to the deep. Richard LAMBERT, who entered on board the Polly at the Cape of Good-Hope, as mate died soon after sailing.

(512) Office of the United Insurance Company, New-York, Feb. 13. Capt. Wm. W. STORY, (Letter) Sir,..Joseph STANSBURY, Sec'ry. New-York, Feb. 15. Capt. Wm. STORY, Sir, I am directed by the Underwriters at the Tontine Coffee-House, in this city, to convey to you their thanks for your spirited behaviour in retaking your vessel from the French prize-master and crew, on your first voyage of last year, in the brig Trio, to Jamaica... John FERRERS. New-York, Feb. 16. Capt. Wm. STORY, Sir,..The President and Directors of the New-York Insurance Company... Daniel PHOENIX, Sec'ry.

(513) Edenton, March 1. Died, the 12th ult. at his seat near Halifax, Col. Nicholas LONG-He is justly lamented by a numerous acquaintance as a valuable and worthy member of society.

(514) Will Be Sold, At the late dwelling house of Col. Thomas HUNTER, dec. on Friday, the 16th of March next, The perishable part of the estate of said deceased... Elisha HUNTER, Jos. RIDDICK, Ex'rs. Gates County, Feb. 26, 1798.

(515) Lands for Sale. On Friday, the 13th day of April next, will be sold, for ready money..at the court-house in Jones county,.. 113,929 acres of land, for taxes..for 1796, lying on the Onslow, Duplin, Lenoir, and Craven county lines, and the head-waters leading from White Oak, Trent and Neuse rivers;..Lands granted to David ALLISON, and was given in as taxable property by Richard BLACKLEDGE, as his agent. Edmund HATCH, Sheriff. January 30, 1798.

(516) James T. WARD, Physician and Surgeon, Offers his services to the public in general..ten years residence with Dr. RAMCKE.. He occupies the house of Captain BENNET, nearly fronting Major ALLEN's. Edenton, January 3, 1798.

(517) Advertisement. Will be Sold, at the late dwelling house of James CAMPBELL, dec..the 26th and 27th days of this instant, All the perishable part of the estate of said deceased... Willis SAWYER, Ex'r. February 14, 1798. N. B. On one of the above days will be rented out..the valuable plantation called Mount Gold, whereon the said James CAMPBELL deceased, formerly lived... John CAMPBELL, Guardian.

(518) Taken by execution, and will be Sold..on..the fourth day of May next..on the premises, the land and improvements, where Mr. Benjamin JONES now lives, in Pasquotank county, supposed to contain upwards of 1000 acres; to satisfy a judgement lately obtained in our Circuit Court, at Raleigh, by Messrs. SHIRTLISS (or SHIRTLIFF) and AUSTIN, against Nathaniel PAYNE and Benjamin JONES. Michael PAYNE, Marshal, North-Carolina District. Edenton, Feb. 8, 1797.

Vol. XIII. THURSDAY, May 10, 1798. Number 642.

(519) Edenton, May 10. William B. GILES, Samuel J. CABELL, and John CLOPTON, members of the House of Representatives..from the state of Virginia, have had leave of absence.

(520) Appointment. Francis HAWKS, of Newbern, is appointed Clerk of the District and Circuit Courts of the United States for the North-Carolina district, in the room of Ab. NEALE, resigned.

(521) From Newbern, April 28. We grieve in having to relate.. after the discovery of the assassination of Mr. BYRNE..his former partner Mr. Stephen CAMBRELENG..(was) unable to account for the facts which pointed him out as the author of the atrocious deed. On Sunday morning he was apprehended, examined, and disharged.. another warrant was issued, on which he was brought before..Magistrates..and committed. On Tuesday morning the prisoners..discovered him in agony..and convulsion..and between the hours of 9 and 10 he expired. A Coroner's inquest..finding that he killed himself by drinking a quantity of liquid laudanum, out of a three

(521) (Cont.) ounce phial, which was found near his corpse.

(522) Notice. At a meeting of the Magistrates, the Commissioners of Navigation, and the Commissioners of the town of Edenton, at the house of Mr. John HORNIBLOW, on this day, it was resolved, That inoculation for the Small Pox in the said town should cease to morrow the 6th inst.-It was also agreed..that Nathaniel ALLEN, Henderson STANDIN and Henry WILLS, should be appointed a committee to give notice to the inhabitants of the adjacent counties of the above resolution..that after the day aforesaid, no person coming from any of the counties or elsewhere would be suffered to be inoculated in the said town..that out of nearly a thousand persons inoculated in the town of Edenton, there have died but three of the Small-Pox, two of whom were suckling infants, and the other under four years of age. Nathaniel ALLEN, Henderson STANDIN, Henry WILLS. Edenton, May 5th, 1798. Since the above date, another person (Wm. WILLIAMS) has died; a man considerably advanced in years, and of very infirm state of body for some time previous to his inoculation. May 9th, 1798.

(523) Mr. BURGESS, Sadler, Has just received from New-York, a handsome assortment of Saddles and Bridles... He occupies the house next door to King LUTEN's store. Edenton, May 10, 1798.

(524) Lands For Sale. At the request of Richard BLACKLEDGE, in behalf of the owners of the 46,720 acres of Land, granted to David ALLISON, in Carteret county..postponed the sale..until..the 17th of May, 1798... Wm. THOMSON, Sheriff. Carteret County, April 11, 1798.

(525) Lands For Sale. At the request of Richard BLACKLEDGE, in behalf of the owners of the 210,260 acres of Land, granted to David ALLISON, in Onslow county..sale..is postponed until..the 11th day of May next... Lemuel DOTY, Sheriff. Onslow County, April 9, 1798.

(526) Spring Goods, Just arrived, and for Sale, by MOODY and AVERY...

(527) Lands For Sale. At the request of Richard BLACKLEDGE, in behalf of the owners of the 128,639 acres of Land, granted to David ALLISON, in Jones county..sale..is postponed until..the 15th day of May ensuing... Edmund HATCH, Sheriff. Jones County, April 9, 1798.

Vol. XIII. THURSDAY, May 24, 1798. Number 644.

(528) Instructions, To Charles C. PINCKNEY, John MARSHALL, and Elbridge GERRY, Envoys Extraordinary and Ministers Plenipotentiary to the French Republic... Timothy PICKERING, Secretary of State.

(529) New-York, May 7. Agreeably to the previous public notice, a meeting of young men of the city of New-York,..assembled on Saturday evening the 5th inst. at GAULTIER's assembly room in William street..pledging themselves to be in readiness at a moment's

(529) (Cont.) warning to obey the summons of their country in repelling at all hazards the threatened dissolution of her constituted authorities. The..meeting was opened..by Samuel JONES, jun. Esq...

(530) New-York, May 11. Duel!!! On Tuesday evening, Mr. JONES met Mr. Blockholst LIVINGSTON on the Battery, walking with his wife and three children. Mr. JONES conceiving himself insulted by a paragraph which appeared in the Argus that morning..written by Mr. LIVINGSTON..a verbal challenge was given by Mr. LIVINGSTON, and accepted by Mr. JONES..the gentlemen met yesterday evening at 6 o'clock, at Hoebuck.. Both fired at the same instant;—Mr. JONES fell and received a mortal wound. (The paragraph.) We understand that at a meeting of the youths of this city, which was held at GAULTIER's Tavern, Col. Nicholas FISH, a stripling of about 48 years, was chosen Chairman.. We also hear, that Master Jemmy JONES, another boy, not quite 60, graced the Assembly with his presence...

(531) Salem, May 8. Extract of a letter from Mr. Henry PHELPS, of Gloucester, to the Editor, dated May 6. "Capt. Joshua WOODBURY arrived here this afternoon, (Sunday) 45 days from Bourdeaux..."

(532) Norfolk, May 8. Counterfeit Notes!! Yesterday a man named James SMITH, was detected in this Borough in the act of passing counterfeit Bank Notes...

(533) Edenton, May 24. Died, on Saturday last, greatly regretted, Mrs. Penelope BENBURY, consort of Gen. Richard BENBURY, of this county.

(534) Advertisement. Taken out of the subscriber's desk some time in..April, a Note of Hand, for 500 dollars, given by Thomas HUNTER, principal; and Matthew BRANTLEY, security, given in favour of the subscriber..dated December 19th 1797, payable the first of April ensuing. This is to forwarn any person from trading for the same... John KITTRELL. Bertie county, May 15, 1798.

(535) BALDERSON & CORNTHWAIT, At their wholesale and retail Grocery Store, On the lower end of Calvert-Street, near the Head of County-Wharf Dock, Baltimore...

(536) James BURGESS, Saddler. Has just received from New-York, a handsome assortment of Saddlery.. He occupies the house next door to King LUTEN's store. Edenton, May 10, 1798.

(537) Jonathan JACOCKS, Has a Brick House, 30 feet square, with three floors, situate on Walnut Point, near Albemarle Sound, about 2 miles from his ferry..open on the 15th of May next, for the reception of such persons as are desirous of having the Small Pox. Boarding and lodging, with attendance and medicine, will be Ten Dollars for each white or free person, and Six Dollars for each slave... Bertie County, April 2d, 1798.

(538) Dismal Swamp Canal. At a meeting of the Directors of the Dismal Swamp Canal Company, May 3d, 1798... Thomas NEWTON, August-

(538) (Cont.) ine SLAUGHTER, John KEARNES, Directors.

(539) Forty Dollars Reward. A Negro Man the property of the Subscriber, near Kingston, run away about 16 months ago,..about 6 feet high, 28 to 30 years of age, well built and stout, very black and good features,..a large full head of hair, speaks loud and strong, and can read print very well; he is a native of Maryland, and..his right name is JOB, but he has altered it to that of DAVID DAVE... Joseph KING.

(540) Murry she's took to the woods, And from me ran away,
The Devil did possess her, She would no longer stay.
This runaway MURRY, I bought from Mr. John VAIL, in Edenton, about two months ago. She is about 40 years old, of a black colour, somewhat inclined to fat.. I will give Ten Dollars to any one who will bring her home to me living in Plymouth... Leven BOZMAN. April 23d, 1798.

Vol. XIII. THURSDAY, May 31, 1798. Number 645.

(541) Edenton, May 31. Appointments by Authority. Joseph HOPKINSON, of Pennsylvania, commissioner for holding a treaty with the Oneida Indians. Winthrop SARGENT, of the north western territory, Governor of the Missisippi territory. John STEEL, of Virginia, Secretary of do. Peter Bryan BRUIN, of the Missisippi territory, to be second Judge of do.. Daniel TILTON, of N. Hampshire, 3d Judge of do.. Gerald BRYAN, of Pennsylvania, 2d mate of a revenue cutter.

(542) Letters remaining in the Post-Office, at Plymouth. Demsey SPRUIL, John FRASIER, John G. ALLEN, Isaac LONG, Simeon NORMON, Coroner of Tyrrell county, Capt. Samuel ARNOLD, Moses INGLEE, David AIRS, John D. WHITE, Elizabeth COMBS, Richard DOWNING, Thomas STURGES, Charles SPRUIL, Benjamin LONG. John ARMISTEAD, P. M.

Vol. XIII. WEDNESDAY EVENING, July 4, 1798. Number 650.

(543) Philadelphia, June 22. On Tuesday last, Benjamin STODDER, Esq. Secretary of the navy, entered on the duties of the department at his office, No. 139, Walnut street.

(544) New-York, June 28. Extract of a letter from Thomas TRUXTON, Esq. to a friend in this town, dated on board the United States frigate Constellation, at sea, 26th June...

(545) Edenton, Wednesday Evening, July 4. The Printer is authorised to inform the inhabitants of the district of Edenton, that Demsey BURGES, Esq. again offers himself a candidate for Representative in Congress.

(546) Died, on Friday last, Mrs. Sarah E. THOMSON.

(547) Died on Monday last, in the neighbourhood of Edenton, Mrs. Elizabeth FLEURY, the wife of Mr. Henry FLEURY. Her exit is generally lamented.

(548) To the Electors for the District of Edenton. The subscriber takes this method of making known his willingness to represent the district of Edenton, in the Congress of the United States... David STONE. Bertie, July 4th, 1798.

(549) State of North-Carolina. Chowan county, June 11, 1798. Notice is hereby given, to all the creditors of John WILLIAMS, of the said county..is dead, and that the subscriber qualified as administrator to the estate of the said deceased, in last June term... Nathan CREECY, Adm.

(550) Ten Dollars Reward. Run away from the subscriber, on the 7th of April last, an old stout negro fellow named DICK PEPPER, a caulker by trade.. He had been run away from November, 1793, till the above date, when I fell in with him..on Ballard's Bridge; upon seizing him he knocked down my servant and endeavoured to get me down, in the presence of one Solomon ELLIOTT.. I bought him November 1793, from William LITTLEJOHN, Esq. Merchant Edenton, from which period he was run away till the 7th April... George MACKENZY. Edenton, July 4th, 1798.

(551) New-York, June 13. Yesterday morning arrived in town from Philadelphia, the honourable James M'HENRY, Secretary of War.

(552) New-York, June 13. Yesterday came on, at the Mayor's court, the trial of those concerned in the late fracas at the gaol-When Ed. JAMISON, Stephen BELKNAP, Thomas KING, Joseph FOWLER, jun., John WATSON, Hugh M'CLURE, Bradford KELLOG, Wm. FOULK, and Wm. KIMBERLY, were convicted of breaking the prison-Reuben WEEKS, Thos. H. HUGHES and Wm. HOGSFLESH-the whole 12, convicted of assaulting Peter LORILLARD with an intent to murder-all of whom, except KELLOG, to be confined to hard labour in the new state prison for 18 months-and KELLOG for one year.

(553) Notice. The Subscriber is no longer a Publican, decent travellers may, nevertheless, get entertainment. William CREECY. Perquimans county, June 21, 1798.

(554) Lost. On Wednesday evening last at Plymouth, A Note of Hand, for 300 Dollars, given by Leven BOZMAN... James TOLER. Plymouth, June 25, 1798.

(555) Notice. All persons indebted to the Subscriber, are desired to be as speedy in their payments as possible..and offers at private Sale, all the property in his possession, consisting of Land, Negroes, Horses, Cattle..&c. &c. Apply to Mr. COLLINS, Edenton, or J. GRANBERY. Gates County, June 13, 1798.

(556) State of North-Carolina. Pasquotank County, June 18, 1798. Notice is hereby given, to all whom it may concern, that Thomas OVERMAN, sen. of the county aforesaid, is dead, and that the subscriber qualified as executor to his estate in March term 1797... Thaddeus FRESHWATER, Ex'r.

(557) State of North-Carolina. Pasquotank County, June 18, 1798.

(557) (Cont.) Notice is hereby given, to all whom it may concern, that Zachariah PENDLETON, of the county aforesaid, is dead, and that the subscriber qualified as administrator to his estate in September term 1797... Thaddeus FRESHWATER, Adm.

(558) State of North-Carolina. Pasquotank County, June 18, 1798. Notice is hereby given, to all whom it may concern, that John PRITCHARD is dead, and that Sarah PRITCHARD qualified as executrix, in March term, 1798, and gave the subscriber a power of attorney to transact the business in her stead... Thaddeus FRESHWATER, for the Ex'x.

(559) State of North-Carolina. Pasquotank County, June 18, 1798. Notice is hereby given, to all whom it may concern, that John NICHOLSON, of the county aforesaid, is dead, and that the subscriber qualified as administrator to his estate in the last June term... Thaddeus FRESHWATER, Adm.

(560) Run away from the Subscriber, a yellow fellow, by the name of _____ ... William STUBBS. Tyrrell County, May 31, 1798.

(561) Academy. Marquis DE CLUGNEY..have removed to the house lately occupied by Mrs. POLLOK, where they propose teaching..vocal and instrumental Music, Dancing and Drawing; also the French language... Edenton, June 20th, 1798.

Vol. XIII. WEDNESDAY EVENING, July 18, 1798. Number 652.

(562) Norfolk, July 12. In consequence of the nomination by the President and Senate of the illustrious veteran George WASHINGTON, Esq. to the chief command of the armies of the United States, the different volunteer corps in this Borough paraded on Wednesday evening, and fired 16 rounds.

(563) Edenton, Wednesday Evening, July 18. To the Electors of the county of Chowan, Notice is hereby given, that I offer myself a Candidate to represent the said county in the House of Commons, at the next General Assembly. Thomas BROWNRIGG. Chowan, July 16th, 1798.

(564) Edenton District, Court of Equity, April Term, 1798. George WEST, Complainant, against The Executors of Cullen POLLOK, dec., defendants..unless Thomas POLLOK, and George POLLOK, two of the Executors..put in their joint or several answers..before next term ..on sixth day of October..said bill will be taken pro confesso against them.. Witness Thomas IREDELL, Clerk and Master for the said court at Edenton, the 20th day of April, Anno Dom. '98. Thomas IREDELL, C. M. Edenton, July 14, 1798.

(565) Medicines..for sale..store of C. W. JANSON, Edenton.

(566) Sheriff's Sales. Lands situated in Gates county..whereof no lists were given in by the proprietors for the year 1797, and whereon the taxes of that year remain unpaid, 4000 acres in the Dismal Swamp, supposed to be the property of Wm. DUVAL, in..Virginia;

(566) (Cont.) 5000 acres in the Dismal Swamp..property of James FONTAINE, in..Virginia; 1185 acres in the Dismal Swamp..property of Edward FONTAINE; 3000 acres in the Dismal Swamp..property of John FONTAINE, in..Virginia; 800 acres on Chowan river, the upper side of Sarum creek, the property of John BROWN, in Southampton county, Virginia; 800 acres on Chowan river, near the road that leads across the river to Winton, the property of the Mr. DICKSONS, of Hertford county. 330 acres on or near Chowan river, on the upper side of the road that leads to Winton, the property of Wm. WYNN, of Hertford county; 80 acres on Chowan river below Flax-Island, the property of Capt. WELLS & RACHEL, in Virginia... Samuel SMITH, Sheriff. Gates county, July 6th, 1798.

(567) The Subscriber has for Sale, at his store, (on Cheap-Side, No. 7) a general assortment of Manufactured Tobacco... R. A. SQUIRES. Edenton, July 11, 1798.

(568) Notice. The Subscriber intending to leave the state for a short time, soon after the middle of August next..requests all those to whom he is indebted to bring forward their claims... Myles O'MALLEY. Edenton, July 9, 1798.

(569) James CUNNINGHAM, Barber, Has just received from Philadelphia, the following articles... Edenton, July 10th, 1798.

Vol. XIII. WEDNESDAY EVENING, August 8, 1798. Number 655.

(570) Philadelphia, July 24. A letter from Mr. Daniel CLARK, jun. of New-Orleans, dated on the 14th ult. has been received by the Secretary of State... Department of State, July 23, 1798. Jacob WAGNER, Chief Clerk.

(571) Edenton, Wednesday Evening, Aug. 8. Richard Dobbs SPAIGHT, Esq. is elected a Representative in Congress for the tenth or Newbern division, in the room of Nathan BRYAN, Esq. deceased.

(572) Appointment Of Commissioners under the act to provide for the valuation of Lands and Houses, and for the enumeration of Slaves. North Carolina 1st division John SKINNER, 2d division Spyers SINGLETON, 3d Joseph J. WILLIAMS, 4th Absalom TATOM, 5th Thomas HENDERSON, 6th Wallace ALEXANDER, 7th Joseph DIXON.

(573) The Committee appointed by the Magistrates, Commissioners of Navigation, and Commissioners of the town of Edenton, are happy in communicating to the public..that they need be under no apprehension of taking the Small-Pox by visiting the town... Nathaniel ALLEN, Henderson STANDIN, Henry WILLS. Edenton, August 5th, 1798.

(574) The subscriber intending to leave this place for New-York, sometime in the beginning of September, intreats, such as owe.. to make payment immediately... Henry WILLS. Edenton, August 8th, 1798.

(575) Notice. That on the 10th day of September next, at the Court-House in Germantown, in the county of Hyde, will be sold..

(575) (Cont.) lands..as much as will pay the taxes..for..1797; 596 acres lying on the head of Pungo river, belonging to the heirs of Thomas JONES, dec. of Beaufort county; 200,000 acres in Pungo Great Dismal, supposed to belong to John HALL; 8000 acres on the head of Pungo river, the property of Josiah COLLINS, of Edenton; 350 acres on Smith's Creek, Currituck, belonging to Elizabeth SYLVESTER, of Virginia; 140 (?) acres on the north dividing creek, supposed to belong to the heirs of James ALDERSON, deceased; 150 acres on Sinclair's creek, belonging to William PRICE; 596 acres lying on Swan quarter, supposed to belong to Thomas PARKER, 2560 acres lying on the north side of Mattemuskeet Lake, supposed to belong to John SMITH, of Baltimore; 320 acres in the Laurel swamp, near Woodstock, belonging to Raphael THOMPSON... Zachariah SPENCER, Sheriff. July 16th, 1798.

(576) Five Dollars Reward. Run Away from the subscriber on the 22d of July, a mulatto man named JACOB DUN, about 45 years of age, 5 feet 7 or 8 inches high; he is free born, and was bound to me... Hillery SANSBURY. August 1, 1798.

(577) Letters remaining in the Post-Office, at Edenton, July 1st, 1798. Thomas ASHBURN, William ASHBURN, Eliash (?) ASHBURN, Benjamin ATKINSON, Martha BRITT, Arthur BROWN, & Co., James BAKER, Absolum BOSTWICK, John BURCHER, Mrs. BRIMAGE, William BUCHANAN, Messrs. Archibald BELL, Joseph SMITH, John BORITZ and Francis HARDY, David KERR, BIXBY & KIETH, Marmaduke KIMBROUGH, Capt. Elias HULEN, 2, Benjamin BRICKELL, John COOPER, Gates, Mrs. Winifred COOK, Capt. John JEALLEN, James CAMOCK, Michael LACOLESS, James CLARY, John COWPER, Pitch-Landing, Clerk of the Superior Court, J. CRICHLOW, J. DEAN, 3, Lockett DAVIS, Christopher DUDLEY, Samuel L. DAVIS, Mons. DAVEJAC, William EDWARDS, William EARL, James EELFUR (or EELSUR), Jeremiah ELLIOTT, Capt. Nathaniel GAGE, Adam GASKINS, John GILES, John GRAHAM, Messrs. John and Thomas HILL, Henry HARRAMOND, 2, Mrs. Gracy HARVEY, Thomas HANKINS, John HORNIBLOW, 2, John LENOX, Archibald M'DUGALD, Niel M'NEEL, Archibald M'NEEL, John M'IVER, Exum NEWBY, 2, Daniel PIERCE, Ivey PURDIE, Samuel PEPPER, Samuel PEACOCK, Job PARKER, Capt. James PARSONS, Solomon PENDER, Daniel RAY, David PRICE, Nicholas REED, Charles SPOONER, Capt. Charles PARSONS, Capt. Thomas SPARKES, James FOULTOWN, MARQUAND and STURGES, John and Thomas FENLEY, William THOMPSON, Mrs. THOMAS, Nancy THOMAS, Capt. William TUYLER, James WARD, Capt. Geo. WEST, William WARBUTTON, Joshua WIRE, Capt. Tilley WENTWORTH, John WALMSLEY, Michael WARD. Henderson STANDIN, P. M.

(578) The late imported horse Silver, is now in full perfection, and will be removed from Halifax county to Salmon Creek, near the Tombstone... John DREW, jun.

(579) State of North-Carolina. Perquimans county, July 29, 1798. Notice is hereby given, to all the creditors of Gen. William SKINNER, dec. late Commissioner of Loans of said State..is dead, and that the subscribers qualified as Executors to his estate, in February term... John HARVEY, Wm. BLOUNT, Wm. WHEATON, Ex'rs.

(580) 20 Dollars Reward. Run away from the subscriber, a negro

(580) (Cont.) fellow named TOM, about 5 feet 8 or 10 inches high, about 25 years of age, very black.. The fellow is well known in Edenton, and has a Mother living there. The above reward,..if delivered to me at Pollok's Ferry, or one half if he is confined in any jail,..or to Thomas SATTERFIELD in Edenton... Shadrach COLLINS. July 29th, 1798. N. B. It is supposed he is lurking about Mr. William LITTLEJOHN's quarter, in Duren's Neck, Perquimans county.

(581) Four Dollars Reward. Run Away from the subscriber on the 11th instant, a yellow negro slave, about 20 years old, named SIP, has been to sea... George MACKENZY. Edenton, July 24th, 1798.

Vol. XIII. WEDNESDAY EVENING, August 29, 1798. Number 658.

(582) Boston, August 9. Captain Albert SMITH, arrived here last evening in 70 days from St. Petersburg (in Russia).

(583) Edenton, Wednesday Evening, Aug. 29. Members of Congress chosen at the late Election. Halifax-Willis ALSTON. Newbern-Richard Dobbs SPAIGHT. Wilmington-William H. HILL. Further returns of Members of Assembly. Hertford-Thomas WYNNS, Senate. Robert MONTGOMERY and James JONES, Commons. New-Hanover-J. BLOODWORTH, Senate. A. D. MOORE and Jas. LARKINS, Commons. Town of Wilmington-James WALKER. Brunswick-Gen. SMITH, Senate. ___ BEZANT and Benjamin MILLS, Commons. Bladen-Josiah LEWIS, Senate. Jas. BRADLEY and S. ASHFORD, Commons. Duplin-J. T. RHODES, Senate. S. STALLINGS and T. KEENAN, Commons. Sampson-J. BLACKMAN, Senate. J. THOMPSON and K. BRYAN, Commons. Cumberland- ___ M'LEAN, Senate. S. PURVIANCE and N. SMITH, Commons. Town of Fayetteville-T. DAVIS. Craven-Lewis BRYAN, Senate. W. BLACKLEDGE and Philip NEALE, Commons. Town of Newbern-John STANLEY. Jones-William BUSH, Senate. Benjamin FORDHAM and Amos JOHNSON, Commons. Granville-William P. LITTLE, Senate. Sterling YANCEY and John R. EATON, Commons. Warren-John WARD, Senate. James TURNER and Oliver FITT, Commons. Franklin-Jordan HILL, Senate. John FOSTER and Archibald DAVIS, Commons. Wake-Thomas HINES, Senate. John ROGERS and John HUMPHREYS, Commons. Nash-John ARRINGTON, Senate. John H. DRAKE and Redmond BUNN, Commons. Edgcomb-Nathan MAYO, Senate. Jeremiah HILLIARD and Adam HAYWOOD, Commons. Pitt-Frederick BRYAN, Senate. Holland JOHNSON and Richard EVANS, Commons. Martin-Samuel JOHNSTON, Senate. Thos. WIGGINS and Jeremiah SLADE, Commons.

(584) Mr. LAILSON most respectfully informs the Ladies and Gentlemen of Edenton, that he will perform on Thursday evening next.. The Famous Horse Bucephalus, will leap through a Hogshead with both ends closed with paper, in full speed, at the command of his rider.. Tickets to be had at Capt. COX's Tavern.

(585) Notice. To be sold, on Saturday, the 15th day of September next, at the Court-House in Tyrrel county, if the taxes are not paid before that day..for the year 1797..viz. 100,000 acres, on the east side of Great Alligator, patented by John G. BLOUNT, and supposed to be owned by Robert MORRIS, of...Philadelphia; 50,000 acres, on the west side of Great Alligator, supposed to be patented

(585) (Cont.) and owned by John G. BLOUNT, as it is entered in his name; 610 acres, in Little Alligator, given in by John Lewis BOYCE; 228 acres, on Little Alligator, supposed to belong to the Heirs of Thomas BARNES, Known by the name of the Black Walnut land. E. BLOUNT, Sheriff.

(586) 20 Dollars Reward. Run away from the subscriber, near Edenton, N. C. a negro fellow by the name of YORK, 25 years of age, about 5 feet 11 inches high..he is a good cooper, and a likely, stout, well built fellow, short hair, and keeps it well combed, he speaks good English and is very shrewd.. I do expect he went from here to Norfolk, with a negro fellow belonging to Capt. Ebenezer PAINE, Master of the ship Roanoke... William BENNETT.

Vol. XIII. WEDNESDAY EVENING, October 31, 1798. Number 668.

(587) Boston, October 12. A gentleman..who came from Vermont yesterday, informs..that the notorious and despised Matthew LYON, has been indicted for treasonable expressions, and libellous publications against the government of the U. States, at the circuit court held at Rutland, on the 6th inst. and was to take his trial last Monday.

(588) Salem, Oct. 12. On Wednesday evening Capt. John DEVEREAUX, in the schooner Rambler, arrived at Marblehead, in 35 days from Lisbon...

(589) Edenton, Wednesday Evening, Oct. 31. Married, on Wednesday evening last, Mr. David BLACK to Miss Elsa BENNETT, both of this town. Same evening, Mr. J. JORDAN, of Perquimans, to Miss Catherine BENNETT, of this town.

(590) Bushrod WASHINGTON, of Virginia, is appointed Associate Justice of the Supreme Court of the United States, vice James WILSON, dec...

(591) Letters remaining in the Post-Office, Edenton, October 1st, 1798. Capt. George A. GILLIKIN, Francis ALBERTSON, John ALDERSON, Abraham BROWN, James BAKER, Dominick CABARRUS, T. CHURCH, John DEMPFREY, Nathaniel DOWNS, James DEAN, Sith EASON, Jeremiah ELLIOTT, Henry EELBECK, James FRAME, Hezekiah GORHAM, Martin GRANADE, James GREGORY, Richard HAUGHTON, C. JAUNDUS, James JONES, Tyrrell, Jehu NICHOLS, Capt. James PARSONS, Susannah PAYNTER, Rev. Charles PETTIGREW, Capt. Peter ROSS, Sheriff of Chowan County, 2, Robert RIDDICK, Nicholas REED, Josiah RODDY, Capt. Thomas SPARK, Wm. STITSON, Stephen STAFFORD, Oliver SMITH, Capt. Charles PARSONS, Wm. THOMPSON, jun., John TAYLOR, Mrs. THOMAS, John Thos. FINLEE, Capt. Wm. TYLER, Capt. Tilley WENTWORTH, Capt. Wm. WILLIAMS, Michael WARD, Mons. VEVIER, Angel WARNIER, Ephraim WHITMORE, John WALMSBRY, Joshua WEST, Stephen WATERMAN. Hend. STANDIN, P. M.

(592) State of North-Carolina. Chowan county, October 28, 1798. Notice is hereby given, to all the creditors of Willis ROBERTS, deceased, late of the county aforesaid..is dead, and that the subscriber qualified as administratrix to his estate, in September

(592) (Cont.) term... Sarah ROBERTS, Administratrix.

(593) Run away from the subscriber, a likely negro man named FRANK, of a yellowish complexion, about 30 years of age, and about 6 feet 9 or 10 inches high..he has a free pass, signed David STANDLY and John DAWSON, both of which have been dead this some years past..25 Dollars Reward... Henry SPILLER. Cashie-Neck, Bertie county, Oct. 2, '98.

(594) Twenty Five Dollars Reward. Ran away on Saturday, the 15th inst. from the Subscriber living near Tarborough, in Edgcomb county, (N. C.) a mulatto negro man, about half blooded, named ROBBIN, about 5 feet 6 or 7 inches high, about 35 years of age, well set, and round face, large neck, steps lively..his hair is very short. I bought him of William Johnston DAWSON, of Bertie county, near Edenton (sic)-he is a shoe maker and cooper... Elias BRYAN. September 27, 1798.

(595) Henry FLURY, Has For Sale, At the Ware-House on the head of the Wharf of Nathaniel ALLEN, Esq...Liverpool China, Glass and Crockery Ware...

(596) Doctor John CUNNINGHAM, Informs..that he has just received from New-York..at his shop in Market-street, directly opposite the Post-Office..Drugs and Medicines, Perfumes and Pomatum, and a few groceries...

(597) The Subscriber offers for Sale, his juniper swamp Land, situate in Gates county, between the mouth of Catherine and Bennett's Creeks, supposed to contain about 1000 acres; the greatest part of which is well timbered with good juniper, within half a mile of the river. There is a small canal cut from the mouth of Bennett's Creek, into the swamp..for carrying shingles or other lumber down... James BAKER. August 20, 1798.

(598) Notice. The Directors taking into consideration the great scarcity of cash at this time, have postponed the sale of the delinquent shares in the Dismal Swamp Canal Company, until the 4th Monday next month... Thomas NEWTON, Augustine SLAUGHTER, J. G. MARTIN, Directors. Norfolk, Sept. 10, 1798.

(599) This is to give notice, that on Saturday, the 20th of October next..will be Sold..the Land and Plantation, whereon Aaron BOULTON, dec. formerly lived, containing by the patent 317 acres.. lies on the head of Little Black Walnut, and on the edge of Bucklesbury pocosin, in Bertie county.. Also..will be sold, a Lot in Colerain, on Chowan river, by the heirs of said deceased. September 7th, 1798.

Vol. XIII. WEDNESDAY EVENING, December 26, 1798. Number 674.

(600) Edenton, Wednesday Evening, Dec. 26. Naval Appointments. George CROSS, Esq. of the United States armed brig General Pinckney, to superintend the building of, and command the ship of war at Charleston. Samuel HEYWARD, Esq. Captain of one of the gallies at

(600) (Cont.) Charleston, to command the United States armed brig General Pinckney.

(601) Married, on Thursday evening last, Mr. George WILKINSON, to Miss ____ M____, both of this town.

(602) On Thursday, the 10th day of January next will be Sold, at public sale, all the property in the subscriber's possession, consisting of Land, Negroes, Horses, Cattle, Household and Kitchen Furniture, &c. &c. Twelve months credit will be given, on bond and security payable to Josiah COLLINS. Josiah GRANBERY. Sunsberry, December 3, 1798.

(603) State of North-Carolina. Chowan county, December 18, 1798. Notice is hereby given, to all the creditors of Ann WILLIAMS, deceased, late of the county aforesaid,...is dead, and that the subscriber qualified as administrator to her estate, in December term ... Thomas HANKINS, Administrator.

(604) State of North-Carolina. Chowan county, November 26, 1798. Notice is hereby given, to all the creditors of Capt. Ebenezer NUTTING, deceased, late of the county aforesaid,...is dead, and that the subscriber qualified as administrator to his estate in September term... Joseph BRYAN, Adm.

(605) The subscriber has for sale, at Dishon's Ferry, on Chowan River, 250 barrels whole Herrings... James GREGORY. Gates County, Dec. 4, 1798.

Vol. XIII. WEDNESDAY EVENING, January 2, 1798.(sic) Number 675.

(606) Boston, December 4. Mr. Giles LODGE, merchant, last night ..politely favoured us with the London Gazette Extra, of October 8th...

(607) Columbia, December 7. Yesterday..the Senate and House of Representatives proceeded to the election of a Governor, Lieut. Governor and Senator to Congress.. Honourable Edward RUTLEDGE, was elected Governor. John DAYTON, Esq. Lieut. Governor. The ballots for Senator..Charles PINCKNEY, Esq...was elected.

(608) Edenton, Friday Evening, Jan. 4. The Printing Office is removed to the east end of the town, near the Rope Walk, to the house of Capt. Thomas COX, lately occupied by William SLADE, Esq.. Owing to the removal of the office, this paper could not make its appearance until today.

(609) The subscriber has just received from New-York, an assortment of Dry Goods... Jeremiah GALLOP.

(610) Just received from New-York, and for sale..by Henry WILLS, A small assortment of Dry Goods... Edenton, January 1st, 1799.

(611) Advertisement. On the 23d of November, the subscriber hired a Carriage and Four Horses, to convey Mr. H____ and family, from

(611) (Cont.) Norfolk, in Virginia, to Newbern or Wilmington, in North Carolina, with positive orders to the driver to return direct .. Fearing that some accident has befallen them, will be much obliged to any person who may..inform him by post or otherwise. The driver is named Frederick APT, a German, about 45 years of age; his nose is very crooked, he is about 5 feet 10 or 11 inches high, remarkable thin, and speaks broken English... Adam LINDSAY. Norfolk, Dec. 29, 1798.

(612) State of North-Carolina. Pasquotank County, December 26, 1798. Notice is hereby given, to all the creditors of Michael LAWLESS, deceased..is dead, and that the subscriber qualified as administrator to his estate the last term... William M. LAUND, Adm.

(613) Notice. Whereas William BLACK and David BLACK, lately transacting business in this place, under the firm of William BLACK and Co. did, on the 21st day of October last, resign into the hands of their creditors..in Virginia, their books, accounts..without reserve. The subscriber is now appointed agent..to settle..the said business. David BLACK, Agent for the creditors of Wm. Black and Co.. Edenton, Jan. 2d, 1799.

(614) Letters remaining in the Post-Office, at Edenton, January 1st, 1799. George ARMISTEAD, William BUCKANNON, Miss Sally BATEMAN, John BROTHERS, WYNNS and BRICKELL, Jos. BIXBY, Samuel BROWN, Jos. BUNCH, Levi BATEMAN, Douglas CHAPMAN, John D. COFFIELD, John COOPER, James DEANE, Christopher DUCKET, William DAVIS, Jeremiah ELLIOTT, Caleb ELLIOTT, Hugh FAGAN, John FERRIS, William GRANDY, William GARDNER, Henry GERRISH, John HORNIBLOW, John and Thomas HILL, Thomas H. HARVEY, Richard HOULY, Josiah JORDEN, Arthur JONES, Russell JOSELIN, Darkess JAMES, James KEYS, Vine LEAVENS, Malachi M'KOY, Duncan M'KENZIE, George M'KENZIE, Ebenezer MAGEE, James MOFFET, James M'NULIE, James MOORE, Patsey M'GLOCKLIN, Henry NORMAN, Nathaniel NICKERSON, Mrs. Sarah NEEL, Myles O'MALLEY, Job PARKER, Christopher PALE, Charles PIERCE, Frederick RAMCKE, Thos. RHODES, Charles RANDOLPH, Nicholas REED, John STUART, Lemuel SUTTON, Lydia SCOTT, Stephen STAFFORD, Mrs. THOMAS, John TAGERT, William TAIT, Solomon WHEELER, Michael WARD, Blake B. WIGGENS, Thomas VAIL, John WHITE, John VAIL, Joshua ULVIER, Simson WHITE, William D. WILKINSON. Henderson STANDIN, P. M.

Vol. XIV. WEDNESDAY EVENING, January 23, 1799. Number 672.

(615) (Circular) To the Commanders of armed vessels in the service of the United States, given at the Navy Department, December 29, 1798... Ben. STODDER.

(616) Edenton, Wednesday Evening, Jan. 23. Wm. BLOUNT has been chosen President of the Senate for the state of Tennessee. It is also said, he will be supported for Governor of that state, at the ensuing election.

(617) Died, on Monday night last, Mrs. Phebe BISSELL, consort of Mr. Thomas BISSELL, merchant, of this town.

(618) Advertisement. The Subscriber informs..that he has removed from the stand he occupied last year, to the house of Henry WILLS, where the Printing-Office was formerly kept, where he proposes to keep a Tavern and Boarding-House, under the sign of the United States Arms and the Indian Queen... Thomas COX. Edenton, January 15, 1799.

(619) Sheriff's Sale. Notice..that the following Lands..in the county of Jones, were not given in by any list..for..1797..and so much of the same will be sold..on 17th February, 1799, as..to satisfy the taxes due.. Edmond HATCH, Sheriff. Jones County, North Carolina, November 27th, 1798. 1280 Acres on the head of gum swamp ..near John ISLAR's line. 8320 acres on the north side of white oak river and west side of Hunter's creek..at the mouth of pometer branch..-James WICKS's corner. 640 acres joining the Onslow county line..-John SAUL's corner on the road. 5120 acres on the north side of Trent river,..-Samuel DELIHUNTER's, beginning of his 100 acre patent. 13705 acres on the north side of Trent river and head of Bachelor's creek, beginning at Hezekiah MERRITT's beginning pine of his 100 acre patent. 35200 acres on the south side Trent river, beginning at a tree called, the Royal Oak, the beginning of two patents in the name of Daniel SHINE. 1408 acres on the south side of Trent river, including the head waters of Rattlesnake branch.. the beginning of Jacob JOHNSTON's 200 acre survey, on the head of Tocohoe branch. 1280 acres on the north side of white oak river.. -Joseph HATCH's and Richard JONES's corner. 640 acres, beginning at a pine-Jonathan KEYS' corner of his 250 acre survey. The foregoing Lands appear on record, as the property of David ALLISON, late of Philadelphia. 2280 acres on the north side of white oak river and west side of great branch..-James TAYLOR's corner of a 300 acre survey. 640 acres on the north side of Trent river, on the head of mirey branch, beginning at two laurels standing south 42E.470 poles from MERRITT's and his own beginning of a patent dated 26 December 1794. 1280 acres on the north side of Trent river, near the head of the beaverdam..-Hezekiah MERRITT's third corner of 100 acre survey, dated the 22d day of October, 1782. 1408 acres on the north side of Tocahoe creek, joining the Duplin and Lenoir county line. 1920 acres on the south side of Trent river, and north west side of catfish lake, between the head of mill creek and island creek, beginning at two bays in Mr. George POLLOCK's line of survey of 640 acres. 1408 acres on the south side of Trent river, including the waters of reedy branch and little cypress creek, joining the Onslow county line, beginning.. in said line in John SHINE's line. 2100 acres on the north side of Tocohoe creek on the head of Joshua's branch..-Jacob JOHNSTON's corner. 3180 acres on the north side of white oak river, and southwest side of catfish lake, and on the head of the black swamp ..George POLLOCK's and James LEECH's corner. 1280 acres on the north side of Tocohoe creek, including the head of great branch, beginning at..the second corner of Rachel GERMAN's 450 acre survey. The foregoing lands appear to be granted to David ALLISON; but is reported to be the property of Mr. A. DUBOIT, of..Philadelphia. 1920 acres on the north side of Trent river..the last corner of Willie GURGENUS's 100 acre survey. 640 acres on the north side of Trent river, including black swamp pocosin..-James WESTBROOK's

(619) (Cont.) corner near William MORGAIN's house. 1300 acres ..- Hall JARMAN's corner. 1280 acres... 640 acres on the north side of Trent river, including Heritage's pocosin..-Benjamin DAVIS's beginning in Lenoir county line. 640 acres on the south side of Trent river..Thos. THORNTON's corner. 2560 acres... 640 acres in Dover pocosin... 15360 acres, including the Batchelor's creek and Dover pocosin, beginning at a..corner of his own survey, surveyed by James JOYE. The foregoing lands were granted to David ALLISON; but are reported to be the property of Solomon MARK and Henry BECK. 1540 acres..the property of Joseph LEECH, Esq. in the lake pocosin. 400 acres..the property of George WARD, on white oak river. 400 acres..of James GREEN, patented by John MARKLAND, on the..Trent. 640 acres..of Daniel WEATHERSPOON..in the cypress creek dismal. 500 acres..of the heirs of Samuel HILL .. 100 acres of Isaac BARNOW..in the waters of Trent. 222 acres ..of Martin PHILLYAW, on the waters of Trent. 500 acres..of John SHINE, on the waters of Trent. Edmond HATCH, Sheriff.

(620) Sheriff's Sale. Notice..that the following Lands,..in the county of Onslow, will be sold for the taxes due..for 1797..on 15th day of February, 1799.. Lemuel DOTY, Sheriff. Onslow county, North-Carolina, November 28th, 1798. 59025 Acres..in the Jones county line in white oak pocosin..beginning at the Royal Oak. 78115 acres..on the head of holleyshelter and shaking creek, joining Newhanover county line..the corner of James CARRAWAY's and Daniel WHEATON's land.. 6336 acres..including the Devil's pocosin..on the path leading from Aaron DAVIS's to William KING's. 4220 acres including the back swamp pocosin..at a fence in SHIPPER's line on long ridge. 7040 acres... 704 acres..near NIXON's line. 2112 acres, beginning at Aaron DAVIS's corner..in Duplin county line. 2816 acres... Lemuel DOTY, Sheriff.

(621) Sheriff's Sale. Notice..that the following Lands,..in the county of Bladen, will be sold for the taxes due..for 1797..on the 26th day of February, 1799. T. HARVEY, Sheriff. Bladen county, N. Carolina, December 3, 1798. 9000 Acres... 9600 acres ... 6336 acres... 9350 acres... 1120 acres... 14040 acres... 5120 acres east of Drowning Creek and Rough horn swamp, including RIGHT's, CAMPBELL's, Wynne NANCE's, A. CRIFFIN's, I. FLOWER's, James M'COULSKY's, E. PARKER's, and John YATES' Surveys. 4480 acres... 3840 acres... 17640 acres... 2000 acres... 4200 acres east of Slap-Ass, centrical to Col. DRY's..corner. 1200 acres south of the northwest river joining Brunswick county..east of Fryar's swamp, on the edge of an old road..from Mrs. WHITE's to General BROWN's. 12000 acres... 6236 acres... 52980 acres... 7680 acres beginning at a pine-Hardy BRYAN's upper corner, on the north side of Bryan's swamp. 1000 acres south of the northwest river, between Slade swamp and Welshe's creek..near the upper edge of David CLARK's land. 12550 acres... 20480 acres... 640 acres... 900 acres on the head of Slap-Ass swamp, beginning in the White-Hall road, where HARGROVE's mill path crosses.. All the above were granted by patents to John Gray BLOUNT. 840 acres on the east side of the White Marsh, belonging to John Gray BLOUNT, now tenanted by John SIMPSON and John CLARK, adjoining lands..of Richard HOLMES and the plantation of said CLARK. 1000 acres on

(621) (Cont.) Colley swamp, joining John G. SCULL's line, entered by Alexander M'KENZIE. 1280 acres on Ellis' creek, supposed the property of ___ WEAKLY, 500 acres on Turnbull creek, supposed the property of M. LOPER. 960 acres on the south side of White Marsh, joining the lands of ___ SESSIONS, and ___ FOWKES, late the property of Elizabeth RICHARDS. T. HARVEY, Sheriff.

Vol. XIV. WEDNESDAY EVENING, January 30, 1799. Number 673.

(622) Salem, December 15. Portsmouth, Dec. 22. Arrived in this town, Capt. Chas. TREADWELL, from Guadaloupe...

(623) Philadelphia, Jan. 3. John BROWN is re-elected Senator in Congress for the state of Kentucky, the ensuing term.

(624) Charleston, January 4. Yesterday..arrived the fishing smack, Zeno, Captain SAWYER, in 11 days from Norfolk. On the 29th ult.. off Cape Fear..gale..washed two men overboard.. Two days to previous to this accident, they spoke the ship Fair American, George FORREST, master...

(625) Edenton, Wednesday Evening, Jan. 30. Congress. House of Representatives, Friday, January 11. The following is a copy of the bill reported by Roger GRISWOLD, for the punishment of certain crimes therein specified...

(626) Extract of a letter from Geo. C. MORTON, acting Consul of the United States, at the Havanna, dated there the 18th November, 1798, to the Secretary of State. "By the delegation of Daniel HAWLEY, Esq., I am at present acting as Consul of the United States in this district..."

(627) The Subscriber has just received a quantity of Winward Island Rum and Molasses... James HATHAWAY. Edenton, Jan. 25th, 1799.

(628) Notice. All those indebted..are requested..to make payment, in order to enable us to pay those we are indebted to. Thomas BISSELL and Son.

(629) To Be Rented. Three Fisheries, lying on Chowan river, which were last season occupied by Messrs. HUNTER and WALTON; by Mr. Josiah GRANBERRY, and by Captain WRIGHT... Charles JOHNSON. Bandon, January 24th, 1799.

Vol. XIV. WEDNESDAY EVENING, February 6, 1799. Number 674.

(630) Norfolk, January 31. Private letters in town state, that Henry TAZEWELL, Esq. Senator from this state..had lately died at Philadelphia, after a few hours indisposition.

(631) Salisbury, (N. C.) January 10. On Thursday night (was murdered) Mr. IRELAND..one of the first settlers in the upper end of Iredell county..having no children, was supposed to possess a large sum of money. On the evening of the 7th inst..Lewis COLLINS..William OWEN, have been confined in the jail of this town, under suspicion..of the above murder.

(632) Edenton, Wednesday Evening, Feb. 6. Married, on Sunday evening last, Mr. Henry FLEURY, to Miss Martha HARRIS, both of this town.

(633) Just received from New-York, and for sale, on Cheap-Side.. by Joseph BOZMAN, A Handsome assortment of Dry Goods... February 1st, 1799.

(634) Advertisement. On the first Saturday in March next, will be Sold..in Bertie county, A Valuable Plantation, adjoining the land of Oliver FERRY, in said county... Joseph CARTEY. Bertie county, Feb. 1st, 1799.

Vol. XIV. WEDNESDAY EVENING, February 20, 1799. Number 676.

(635) Edenton, Wednesday Evening. Feb. 20. On Saturday arrived at this port, 4 masters of vessels from Guadalcupe..one of whom has favoured us with the following list of American vessels at Basseterre: Ships-Fortitude, Peter DYER, of Portland, taken 5th October from Portland to Barbadoes. Caroline, Ben. GLAZIER, Newburyport, from Norfolk to St. Vincent's, 23d. Nov. Brigs-James, Geo. BUSCOCK, of New-York, 9th Oct. from Savannah to Martinico. Three-Friends, John INDIGO, from Laguira to Salem, was retaken. Sally, Adam MARSTERS, New-York, 17th Oct. from New-York to Martinico. Schooners-Ranger, Josiah BACON, of Boston, 20 Oct. from Boston to Martinico. Syrus, Jared ARNOLD, of Baltimore, from ditto to Laguira. Hylander, M'CONNELL, from Baltimore bound to Martinico. Katy, Christopher WILLIAMS, of Norfolk, 12th Nov. from Norfolk to St. Thomas. ____, Wm. SMITH, Baltimore to Martinico, 17th Nov. Exchange, Jeremiah GALLOWAY, Alexandria to Martinico. Active, of Wells (Mass.), Obadiah GARRISH, 20th Nov. from St. Vincent's to Wells. Margaretta, Aaron BROCK, 26th Nov. from Norfolk to Martinico. Amelia, Tim HALL, from New-Haven to do., 22d Nov. Polly, A. BURN, from New-Haven. Retaliation, Capt. BENBRIDGE. Sloops-Townsend, Daniel CAMPBELL, Boockbay, 6th Oct. from Boockbay to Antigua. Somerset, WIGGINS, from Port-Royal (Vir.), 8th Nov. to St. Vincent's. Endeavour, Jas. MILLER, Portland, from Surinam to Portland. Fox-Darby, John LUMIN, 16th Nov. from Antigua to New-Haven. Dove, CONNELL, New-York, from Louisiane to New-York. Jan. 28th. Spoke the ship Fame, Chas. DARBY, from Grenada, bound to Boston, out 21 days...

(636) To all whom it may Concern, The Subscriber gives this public notice, that he has been duly appointed..his Swedish Majesty's Vice-Consul, for the state of North-Carolina... John BORRITZ. Edenton, Feb. 18, 1799.

(637) For Sale, The House and Two Lots..where the Subscriber now lives, in the town of Edenton... Michael PAYNE. Edenton, Feb. 18, 1799.

(638) Ten Dollars Reward. Run away from the Subscriber, on the first day of January last, a negro man by the name of HUSE, about 22 years old, 5 feet 8 or 9 inches high, a well built fellow... Elizabeth BOND. February 15, 1799.

(639) For Sale, The House and Lotts, the property of the Subscriber, whereon he now lives... Thomas SEAMAN. Edenton, Feb. 12, 1799.

(640) The Subscriber has for Sale, about 100 barrels Herrings, lying at Dishon's Ferry, on Chowan river. For terms apply to E. and B. NORFLEET, in Edenton, or the Subscriber in Gates County... James GORDON. February 13, 1799.

END OF VOLUME III

APPENDIX

1796

```
JANUARY                    FEBRUARY                   MARCH
S  M  T  W  T  F  S        S  M  T  W  T  F  S        S  M  T  W  T  F  S
            1  2              1  2  3  4  5  6                 1  2  3  4  5
3  4  5  6  7  8  9        7  8  9 10 11 12 13        6  7  8  9 10 11 12
10 11 12 13 14 15 16      14 15 16 17 18 19 20       13 14 15 16 17 18 19
17 18 19 20 21 22 23      21 22 23 24 25 26 27       20 21 22 23 24 25 26
24 25 26 27 28 29 30      28 29                      27 28 29 30 31
31

APRIL                      MAY                        JUNE
S  M  T  W  T  F  S        S  M  T  W  T  F  S        S  M  T  W  T  F  S
            1  2           1  2  3  4  5  6  7                    1  2  3  4
3  4  5  6  7  8  9        8  9 10 11 12 13 14        5  6  7  8  9 10 11
10 11 12 13 14 15 16      15 16 17 18 19 20 21       12 13 14 15 16 17 18
17 18 19 20 21 22 23      22 23 24 25 26 27 28       19 20 21 22 23 24 25
24 25 26 27 28 29 30      29 30 31                   26 27 28 29 30

JULY                       AUGUST                     SEPTEMBER
S  M  T  W  T  F  S        S  M  T  W  T  F  S        S  M  T  W  T  F  S
            1  2              1  2  3  4  5  6                    1  2  3
3  4  5  6  7  8  9        7  8  9 10 11 12 13        4  5  6  7  8  9 10
10 11 12 13 14 15 16      14 15 16 17 18 19 20       11 12 13 14 15 16 17
17 18 19 20 21 22 23      21 22 23 24 25 26 27       18 19 20 21 22 23 24
24 25 26 27 28 29 30      28 29 30 31                25 26 27 28 29 30
31

OCTOBER                    NOVEMBER                   DECEMBER
S  M  T  W  T  F  S        S  M  T  W  T  F  S        S  M  T  W  T  F  S
                  1           1  2  3  4  5                       1  2  3
2  3  4  5  6  7  8        6  7  8  9 10 11 12        4  5  6  7  8  9 10
9 10 11 12 13 14 15       13 14 15 16 17 18 19       11 12 13 14 15 16 17
16 17 18 19 20 21 22      20 21 22 23 24 25 26       18 19 20 21 22 23 24
23 24 25 26 27 28 29      27 28 29 30                25 26 27 28 29 30 31
30 31
```

1797

JANUARY
```
S  M  T  W  T  F  S
1  2  3  4  5  6  7
8  9 10 11 12 13 14
15 16 17 18 19 20 21
22 23 24 25 26 27 28
29 30 31
```

FEBRUARY
```
S  M  T  W  T  F  S
            1  2  3  4
5  6  7  8  9 10 11
12 13 14 15 16 17 18
19 20 21 22 23 24 25
26 27 28
```

MARCH
```
S  M  T  W  T  F  S
            1  2  3  4
5  6  7  8  9 10 11
12 13 14 15 16 17 18
19 20 21 22 23 24 25
26 27 28 29 30 31
```

APRIL
```
S  M  T  W  T  F  S
                     1
2  3  4  5  6  7  8
9 10 11 12 13 14 15
16 17 18 19 20 21 22
23 24 25 26 27 28 29
30
```

MAY
```
S  M  T  W  T  F  S
   1  2  3  4  5  6
7  8  9 10 11 12 13
14 15 16 17 18 19 20
21 22 23 24 25 26 27
28 29 30 31
```

JUNE
```
S  M  T  W  T  F  S
               1  2  3
4  5  6  7  8  9 10
11 12 13 14 15 16 17
18 19 20 21 22 23 24
25 26 27 28 29 30
```

JULY
```
S  M  T  W  T  F  S
                     1
2  3  4  5  6  7  8
9 10 11 12 13 14 15
16 17 18 19 20 21 22
23 24 25 26 27 28 29
30 31
```

AUGUST
```
S  M  T  W  T  F  S
      1  2  3  4  5
6  7  8  9 10 11 12
13 14 15 16 17 18 19
20 21 22 23 24 25 26
27 28 29 30 31
```

SEPTEMBER
```
S  M  T  W  T  F  S
                  1  2
3  4  5  6  7  8  9
10 11 12 13 14 15 16
17 18 19 20 21 22 23
24 25 26 27 28 29 30
```

OCTOBER
```
S  M  T  W  T  F  S
1  2  3  4  5  6  7
8  9 10 11 12 13 14
15 16 17 18 19 20 21
22 23 24 25 26 27 28
29 30 31
```

NOVEMBER
```
S  M  T  W  T  F  S
            1  2  3  4
5  6  7  8  9 10 11
12 13 14 15 16 17 18
19 20 21 22 23 24 25
26 27 28 29 30
```

DECEMBER
```
S  M  T  W  T  F  S
                  1  2
3  4  5  6  7  8  9
10 11 12 13 14 15 16
17 18 19 20 21 22 23
24 25 26 27 28 29 30
31
```

1798

JANUARY
S	M	T	W	T	F	S
	1	2	3	4	5	6
7	8	9	10	11	12	13
14	15	16	17	18	19	20
21	22	23	24	25	26	27
28	29	30	31			

FEBRUARY
S	M	T	W	T	F	S
				1	2	3
4	5	6	7	8	9	10
11	12	13	14	15	16	17
18	19	20	21	22	23	24
25	26	27	28			

MARCH
S	M	T	W	T	F	S
				1	2	3
4	5	6	7	8	9	10
11	12	13	14	15	16	17
18	19	20	21	22	23	24
25	26	27	28	29	30	31

APRIL
S	M	T	W	T	F	S
1	2	3	4	5	6	7
8	9	10	11	12	13	14
15	16	17	18	19	20	21
22	23	24	25	26	27	28
29	30					

MAY
S	M	T	W	T	F	S
		1	2	3	4	5
6	7	8	9	10	11	12
13	14	15	16	17	18	19
20	21	22	23	24	25	26
27	28	29	30	31		

JUNE
S	M	T	W	T	F	S
					1	2
3	4	5	6	7	8	9
10	11	12	13	14	15	16
17	18	19	20	21	22	23
24	25	26	27	28	29	30

JULY
S	M	T	W	T	F	S
1	2	3	4	5	6	7
8	9	10	11	12	13	14
15	16	17	18	19	20	21
22	23	24	25	26	27	28
29	30	31				

AUGUST
S	M	T	W	T	F	S
			1	2	3	4
5	6	7	8	9	10	11
12	13	14	15	16	17	18
19	20	21	22	23	24	25
26	27	28	29	30	31	

SEPTEMBER
S	M	T	W	T	F	S
						1
2	3	4	5	6	7	8
9	10	11	12	13	14	15
16	17	18	19	20	21	22
23	24	25	26	27	28	29
30						

OCTOBER
S	M	T	W	T	F	S
	1	2	3	4	5	6
7	8	9	10	11	12	13
14	15	16	17	18	19	20
21	22	23	24	25	26	27
28	29	30	31			

NOVEMBER
S	M	T	W	T	F	S
				1	2	3
4	5	6	7	8	9	10
11	12	13	14	15	16	17
18	19	20	21	22	23	24
25	26	27	28	29	30	

DECEMBER
S	M	T	W	T	F	S
						1
2	3	4	5	6	7	8
9	10	11	12	13	14	15
16	17	18	19	20	21	22
23	24	25	26	27	28	29
30	31					

1799

JANUARY
```
 S  M  T  W  T  F  S
          1  2  3  4  5
 6  7  8  9 10 11 12
13 14 15 16 17 18 19
20 21 22 23 24 25 26
27 28 29 30 31
```

FEBRUARY
```
 S  M  T  W  T  F  S
                   1  2
 3  4  5  6  7  8  9
10 11 12 13 14 15 16
17 18 19 20 21 22 23
24 25 26 27 28
```

MARCH
```
 S  M  T  W  T  F  S
                   1  2
 3  4  5  6  7  8  9
10 11 12 13 14 15 16
17 18 19 20 21 22 23
24 25 26 27 28 29 30
31
```

APRIL
```
 S  M  T  W  T  F  S
    1  2  3  4  5  6
 7  8  9 10 11 12 13
14 15 16 17 18 19 20
21 22 23 24 25 26 27
28 29 30
```

MAY
```
 S  M  T  W  T  F  S
             1  2  3  4
 5  6  7  8  9 10 11
12 13 14 15 16 17 18
19 20 21 22 23 24 25
26 27 28 29 30 31
```

JUNE
```
 S  M  T  W  T  F  S
                      1
 2  3  4  5  6  7  8
 9 10 11 12 13 14 15
16 17 18 19 20 21 22
23 24 25 26 27 28 29
30
```

INDEX

This work has been indexed to individual item numbers instead of page numbers. Please be aware that there are several different spellings for many of these names. All names beginning with a given letter of the alphabet should be checked.

ABORN, J. 312
ADAMS, ___ 228, 265, 328
  Charles 61
  John 23, 215, 270, 319, 330, 357, 385
  John Q. 392, 395, 429
  John Quincy 389
  Sam. 109
  Samuel 270, 332
ADET, ___ 81
AIRS, David 542
ALBERTSON, Benj. 299
  Francis 591
ALDERSON, J. 348, 420
  James 575
  Jas. 417
  John 591
  Simon 454
ALEXANDER, James 161
  John 396
  Wallace 572
ALLEN, ___ 368, 516
ALLEN, COLLINS and Co. 394
ALLEN, Isaac 405
  John 396
  John G. 542
  N. 495
  Nathaniel 233, 282, 522, 573
ALLISON, David 497, 498, 515, 524, 525, 527, 619
ALSTON, George 317
  Willis 583
ALVES, Walter 444
AMIS, Thomas 296
ANDREWS, Robert 225
ANKERS, John 345
ANSLEY, Joseph 138

APT, Frederick 611
ARCHIBALD, James 426, 470
ARMISTEAD, George 614
  John 291, 300, 542
  Sarah 291
  William 124, 153
  William, Jr. 229
ARMOUR, F. 101
ARMSTRONG, Russell 138
ARNETT, Isaac 104
ARNOLD, Jared 635
  Joseph 138
  Reuben 104, 500
  Samuel 542
ARRINGTON, John 583
ART, ___ 472
ASHBURN, Eliash (?) 577
  Elisha 364
  Thomas 414, 577
  William 577
ASHE, Samuel 65, 161, 278, 454, 467, 503
ASHFORD, S. 583
ASHLY, Abel 222
ASPRAY, John F. 291, 364
ATKINS, Nicholas 364, 426
ATKINSON, Benjamin 104
AUSTIN, ___ 518
AVERY, John, Jr. 350
AVERY, MOODY and 380, 526
AVERY, Park 468
AYLWARD, James 349
BACON, Josiah 635
BADHAM, John 12
BAER, George 249
BAILEY, Thomas 83
BAINS, George, Jr. 221

BAINS (Cont.)
  William 17
BAKER, ____ 500
  Blake 291
  Henry 291, 500
  James 291, 364, 426, 577, 591, 597
  Joseph, Jr. 345
  Law. 58
  Lawrence 104, 364, 390, 426, 470
  Timothy 312
  William 202, 470, 500
BALDERSON & CORNTHWAIT 535
BALDWIN, ____ 100
BALLARD, Jesse 291
  John 291
  K. 58
BANBURY, John 222
BANCROFT, Samuel 285
BANKS, Thomas 441
BARKER, ____ 172
BARNES, Rich. 58
  Thaddeus 446
  Thomas 585
BARNEY, ____ 197
  Joshua 327
BARNOW, Isaac 619
BARR, STUART and 387
BARRY, John 383
BARTOLL, Wm. 500
BARTON, Jeremiah 500
  John 197
BASH, William 454
BATCHELDER, Asa 146
BATEMAN, Levi 614
  Sally 614
  T. 132
  Wm. 500
BATES, S. 364
BATWICK, Isaac 144
BAYARD, Sam. 336
BAYLOR, Jacob, Sr. 161
BEASLEY, Elizabeth 104
BECK, Henry 619
BEDFORD, Thomas 417
BELKNAP, Stephen 552
BELL, Archibald 577
  Bethell 195
  Thomas 91
BEMBRIDGE, Caleb 104
BENBRIDGE, ____ 635
BENBURY, Penelope 533
  Richard 18, 189, 441, 451, 500, 533

BENJAMIN, P. 180
BENNET, ____ 516
  Joseph 222
BENNETT, Amey 410
  Catherine 589
  Elsa 589
  John 410
  Polly 129
  William 129, 586
BENSON, Egbert 269
  Lemuel 277
BENT, Thomas 291
  William 168
BENTON, Myles 144
BERESFORD, ____ 101
BERNARD, Lewis 402
BERR__, John 311
BERRENGER, ____ 222
BERRY, Onan 364
BEZANT, ____ 583
BILLATO, Francis 374
BINFORD, John 446
  John M. 195
BISSELL, Phebe 617
  Thomas 617
  Thomas, and Son 628
BIXBY, ____ 282
BIXBY & KEITH 577
BIXBY, Jos. 614
  Joseph 491
  Nathan 491
BLACHON, Peter 291
BLACK, Alexander 222, 291
  David 589, 613
  William 114, 613
BLACKLEDGE, Richard 497, 498, 515, 524, 525, 527
  W. 583
  Wm. 446
BLACKMAN, J. 583
BLACKWOOD, John 247
BLAIR, ____ 50
BLAKE, Ellis Gray 104
BLODGET, Benjamin 412
BLOODWORTH, J. 583
BLOUNT, ____ 89, 412
  Ann 254
  E. 409, 585
  Edmund 186, 187
  Jacob 216, 254, 305
  John 64, 337, 426
  John G. 409, 585
  John Gray 621
  Joseph 168
  Mary 64

BLOUNT (Cont.)
  Sarah 315
  T. 132
  Thomas 198, 424
  William 70, 119, 128, 195, 364, 424, 426, 432
  Willie 1, 114
  Wm. 291, 579, 616
BLOW, Richard 225
BOARDMAN, ____ 470
BON, ____ 500
BOND, Elizabeth 638
  James 12
BONNER, Joseph 291
BOOKS, Job F. 510
BORITZ, John 577
BORRITZ, John 291, 636
  William 148, 149, 438
BOSTWICK, Absolum 577
BOSWORTH, Obadiah 21, 104
BOUDINOT, Elias 309
BOULTON, Aaron 599
BOURNE, Sylvanus 375
BOYCE, James 104, 281, 391
  John Lewis 585
BOYD, James 263
BOZMAN, Joseph 185, 633
  Leven 463, 540, 554
BRADFORD, ____ 458
BRADLEY, Daniel 426
  James 53, 137
  Jas. 583
  John 256
BRAMS, Zabeech 143
BRANDT, Simeon 478
BRANTLEY, Matthew 107, 534
BRATTEN, Nathaniel 132
BRAZER, John 480
BREDGER, Joseph 143
BREOL, ____ 291
BRICKELL, Benjamin 577
BRICKELL, WYNNS and 614
BRICKHOUSE, William 138
BRICKLE, WYNNS and 364
BRIGGS, William 44, 116
BRIGHT, John 417
BRIMAGE, ____ 21, 168, 577
  Thomas West 470
BRITAIN, William 161
BRITH, Martha 364
BRITT, Martha 577
BROADWELL, Hezekiah 21, 364, 470, 509
BROCK, Aaron 635
BROOK, Robert 257

BROTHERS, John 614
BROUGH, Robert 15, 42, 131, 225, 280, 281, 343, 391
BROWER, Theophilus 368
BROWN, ____ 323, 329, 459, 621
  Abraham 591
  Andrew 322
  Anthony 256
  Arthur 426, 470
  Arthur, & Co. 577
  Geo. 320
  James Henry 426
  John 364, 426, 566, 623
  Joseph A. 222, 226, 231, 476
  Robert 275
  Rynolds 500
  Samuel 614
  Thomas 460
  William 104
  William (?) 263
BROWNRIGG, John 231
  Thomas 143, 226, 231, 476, 563
BRUCE, Charles 296
  Daniel 168
BRUER, William 13
BRUIN, Peter Bryan 541
BRUSS (or BRUFF), James 188
BRYAN, Elias 594
  Frederick 583
  Gerald 541
  Hardy 621
  Joseph 21, 470, 604
  K. 583
  Lewis 583
  Nathan 194, 571
BRYER, ____ 222
BUCHANAN, William 577
BUCKANNON, William 577
BUFFUM, J. 510
BULKLEY (?), Thomas 429
BULLOCK, John 21, 364
BUNCH, Jos. 614
BUNN, E. 454
  Redmond 583
  Redmund 446
BURCHER, John 577
BURGES, Demsey 19, 111, 175, 194, 364, 545
  Zephaniah 441
BURGESS, ____ 523
  James 536
BURKITT, Lemuel 104, 132
BURN, A. 635
BURNETT, John 474

BURR, ____ 265
  Aaron 270, 319
BURT, Joseph 510
BURTON, Robert 225
BUSCOCK, Geo. 635
BUSH, William 583
BUSKMAN, ____ 417
BUTLER, ____ 421
  Pierce 424
  Ryan T. 21
  S. 455
  Samuel 117
BYNUM, ____ 351
BYRNE, ____ 521
CABARRUS, Dominick 591
  Stephen 148, 149
CABB, Samuel 222
CABELL, Samuel J. 519
CABOT, S. 363
  Samuel 480
CALDWELL, ____ 444
  Henry G. 84
CALHOUN, James 327
CALLAGHAN, Daniel 473
CAMBRELENG, Stephen 521
CAMERON, John 21
CAMOCK, James 577
  James, and Co. 130
CAMPBELL, ____ 86, 621
  Alexander 120
  Colin 426
  Daniel 635
  James 21, 364, 517
  John 287, 517
  Laurence 159
CANNON, Jesse 394
CANTINE, Peter, Jr. 246
CAPEHART, Michael 364
CARBOT, S. 261
CAREY, ____ 323
  Mary 222
CARMER, James 364, 426, 500, 509
CARNEY, S. W. 195
  Stephen 446
CARPENTER, Stephen 251
  Thomas 335
CARRAWAY, James 620
CARRINGTON, George 296
CARROLL, John 104
CARRUTHERS, Margaret 426
CARTER, James 437
  Landon 114
  Moore 58
  Sally 364

CARTFY, Joseph 634
CARTWRIGHT, Timothy 144
CARY, Mary 291
CASE, John P. 291
  John Peek 88
CASTEN, ____ 341
CASWEL, ____ 345
CATHCART, James L_nder 429
CAVAUGH, Hugh 500
CHAMBERLAIN, E. 364
  Ralph 364
CHAMBERLAN, John 470
CHAPMAN, Douglas 470, 614
CHARLES, Susannah 168
CHARLTON, Jasper 11, 118, 168
CHASE, Samuel 50, 86
CHASTAIN, ____ 487
CHESSON, S. 138
CHEW, James 21, 291
CHILDS, F. 429
CHURCH, John 489
  T. 591
  Thomas C. 337
  Wm. 500
CLANNEL (?), Benjamin 3
CLARE, ____ 331
CLARK, Daniel, Jr. 570
  David 364, 621
  Hester 21
  Isaac 426
  John 621
  Samuel (?) 474
  Thomas 21
CLARKE, Thomas 222
CLARKSON, Samuel R. 364
CLARY, James 577
CLAYLAND, DOBBIN & Co. 327
CLAYTON, John 138
CLEAVES, James 417
CLEMONS, William 163
CLERK, ____ 477
CLEVELAND, ____ 174
CLINTON, George 270
CLOPTON, John 78, 519
COATES, John H. 272, 340, 364
COBBETT, William 324
  Wm. 362
COCKE (?), William 128
COFFIELD, Benjamin 144, 189, 441
  John D. 614
COFFIN, ____ 224
  Hiram 481
COHOON, Gideon 138
COIT, Elisha 468

COIT (Cont.)
   William 468
COLE, Asia 240
   Wm. 481
COLEFAX, William 247
COLEMAN, Robert 263
COLES, John B. 346
COLLINS, ____ 555
COLLINS, ALLEN and Co. 394
COLLINS, Josiah 254, 575
   Lewis 631
   Shadrach 580
   Thomas 104
COLQUHOUN, James 296
COLUMBUS, Christopher 68
COMBES, John Joseph 300
COMBS, Elizabeth 542
   John Joseph 243
CONN, Edward 500
CONNELL, ____ 635
CONNER, John 404
COOK, Shubal 13
   Thomas 168
   Winifred 577
COOKLIN, ____ 157
COOPER, ____ 183
   John 577, 614
   Susan 21
COOR, James 290
COPELAND, DREW and 130
COPELAND, Henry 104
CORNELL, Gideon 364
CORNTHWAIT, BALDERSON & 535
COVERLY, Samuel, Jr. 426
COWARD, William 489
COWPER, John 168, 222, 364, 577
COWPERTHWAIT, J. 373
COX, ____ 584
   John 364, 472
   Thomas 507, 608, 618
COXE, Tenche 490
CRAFFTS, W. & E. 327
CRAICK, Wm. 249
CRAVEN, J. 209
   John 278
CRAWFORD, James 222
   William 222
   Wm. 291
CRAY, Joseph S. 454
CREECY, Lemuel 189, 221, 441
   Nathan 549
   Thomas 177
   William 553
CRICHLOW, J. 577

CRIFFIN, A. 621
CROP, CYPR. 58
CROPTON, John 352
CROSS, George 600
CROWNENSHIELD, Jacob 485
CRUFT, John 382
CUMMING, Hugh 426
   William 384, 408
CUNNINGHAM, ____ 9
   James 569
   John 308, 407, 596
CUSHING, ____ 79
   John 55
   Robert 291, 364
   William 50, 86
CUTLIP, Matthias 41
DAILETT, Anthony 291
DAILY, Enoch 195
   William 218
DAKINGS, Joseph, and Co. 250
DAL VACHO, Batis 470
DALE, Richard 383
DALEY, Enoch 441
DALGLISH, James 273
DANA, Fran__s 413
   Francis 395
DANDRAGE, ____ 351
DARBY, Chas. 635
DAUGE, Willoughby 434
DAUGHTRY, Myles 143
DAVEJAC, ____ 577
DAVENPORT, Frederick 138
   George 417
   Joel 417
DAVID, Claudius 87, 164
DAVIE, W. R. 104, 203
   William R. 195, 427
DAVIS, Aaron 620
   Archibald 583
   Benjamin 619
   E., and Son 261, 363
   Goodoram 296
   John 171
   John D. 426
   Lockett 577
   Samuel L. 577
   T. 583
   William 614
DAVOZAC, ____ 500
DAVY, William 433
DAWSON, John 352, 593
   P. 182
   Penelope 425
   William F. 182
   William J. 470

DAWSON (Cont.)
   William Johnston 25, 594
DAY, Benjamin 225
DAYTON, John 607
DE CALMETZ, Jean Mathiese 149
DE CLUGNEY, ____ 466, 470, 561
DE LERTIER, Calmetz 148, 149
DE NARD, ____ 470
DE NEUFVILLE, John 349
DE SERCEY, ____ 470
DE WITT, Simeon 160
DEAN, J. 577
   James 591
DEANE, James 614
DEARBORN, Henry 245
DELANE, ____ 511
DELIHUNTER, Samuel 619
DELVAUX, ____ 71
DEMPFREY, John 591
DENNIS, John 249
DENT, George 249
DERBY, Abner 104
DEVEREAUX, John 588
DEVEREUX, John 364
DEWAR, David 36
DIAMOND, Benjamin 321
DICKINSON, J. F. 107
   Samuel 88
DICKSON, Probard 104
DICKSONS, ____ 566
DINSMOOR, Silas 89
DIROLL, Stephen 168
DIXON, Joseph 572
DNOFER (?), Willes 138
DOBBIN, CLAYLAND, & Co. 327
DOGGATE, ____ 46
DONALDSON, Andrew 192
   Joseph 43
   Joseph, Jr. 90
   Robert 184
   Samuel 202
DONE (?), Israel 314
DORSEY, Leven 372
DOTY, Lemuel 498, 525, 620
DOUGHTIE, William 58
DOUGLAS, William 225
DOWNING, Richard 542
   William 143
DOWNS, Nathaniel 426, 591
DRAKE, John H. 583
DREW and COPELAND 130
DREW, John, and Co. 21
   John, Jr. 506, 578
   John, Sr. 506
   Seth 28

DREW (Cont.)
   William 130
DRY, ____ 621
DUBOIS, ____ 168, 492
   Jonathan 426
DUBOIT, A. 619
DUBOYCE, ____ 27
DUCKENFIELD, ____ 29
DUCKET, Christopher 614
DUCKITT, Christopher 104
DUDLEY, Christopher 454, 577
DUGEON, John 31
DUGUID, Alex. 206
DUNLAP, James 54
DUNN, Robert 388
DUNSCOMB, James 21, 83, 470
DUPUY, ____ 104
DUVAL, Wm. 566
DYER, Peter 635
EAGAN, ____ 218
EARL, Ann 216, 217
   William 577
EARLE, Nancy 167
EASON, Sith 591
EATON, John R. 583
   William 429
ECCLESTON, ____ 388
EDGAR, Hayden 426
EDMUNDS, Nicholas 446
   William 256
EDWARDS, William 577
EELBECK, ____ 258
EELFUR (or EELSUR), James 577
EGAN, ____ 30
   Robert 12, 20, 92, 117, 118,
      232, 272, 301, 340
   Sarah 20
ELLBECK, Henry 591
ELLERSON, Thomas 417
ELLICOT, Andrew 423
ELLIOT, Caleb 222
   George 178
ELLIOTT, Caleb 614
   Jeremiah 577, 591, 614
   Solomon 550
ELLIS, William 21, 44, 116
ELLISON, Thomas 441
ELLSWORTH, ____ 370
   Oliver 79
ELSBRE, Ephraim 394, 396, 417
ENGS, E. Sarah 39
EPPES, ____ 86
ESTICK, Isaac 314
ETHERIDGE, Thomas 74
EVANS, Francis 143

EVANS (Cont.)
  Griffith 401
  John 472
  Michael 29
  Michael C. 136
  Richard 583
  Venice 470
EVERITT, Thomas 138
FAGAN, Hugh 614
  William 144
FARANGE, William 441
FARROW, Mary 360
FARTHAUTS, J. P. 12
FENLEY, John 577
  Thomas 577
FENNELL, Michael 434
FENNO, ___ 67
FEREBEAU, ___ 298
FEREBEE, Joseph 193, 195
  Samuel 193
  Thom. C. 144
FERGUSON, Alexander 364
FERRERS, John 345, 512
FERRIS, John 614
FERRY, Oliver 634
FIELD, Hume R. 296
FIGURES, Matt. 16
FINCH, Hugh 470
  James 291
  John Allen 458
FINLEE, John Thomas 591
FISH, Nicholas 530
FISHER, William 184
FISK, James 495
FITT, Oliver 583
FITZSIMONS, Thomas 67, 96
FLAGG, ___ 244
FLEURY, Elizabeth 547
  Henry 632
FLOURNOY, Robert 84
FLOWERS, I. 621
FLURY, Henry 168, 595
FONTAINE, Edward 566
  James 566
  John 566
FORBES, Lemuel 132
FORDHAM, Benjamin 583
FORREST, George 624
FORRESTER, ___ 345
FOSTER, ___ 314, 368
  John 454, 583
FOULK, Wm. 552
FOULTOWN, James 577
FOWKES, ___ 621
FOWLER, Joseph, Jr. 552

FOWLER (Cont.)
  Stephen 21
FOX, Josiah 430
FRAME, James 426, 591
FRASIER, John 542
FRASIR, James 168
FRATER, John 21
FRAZOR, John 364
FREEMAN, James 58
FRELENGHUYSEN, Frederick 100
FRESHWATER, Thaddeus 212, 556, 557, 558, 559
FRUNSON, James 138
FURLONG, ___ 363
GAGE, Nathaniel 577
GALLATIN, Albert 183
GALLAWAY, James 225
GALLOP, Jeremiah 150, 386, 450, 609
GALLOWAY, Jeremiah 635
GARDNER, Benjamin 337
  William 614
GARRET, Thomas 426
GARRETT, Joseph 104
GARRISH, Obadiah 635
GASKINS, Adam 577
GATLING, James 195
  Jas. 454
GAULTIER, ___ 529
GAUZAN, ___ 291
GAYLE, Christopher 104
GERMAN, Rachel 619
GERRISH, Henry 614
GERRY, Elbridge 413, 528
GILBERT, ___ 454
GILELAND, Mary 426
GILES, Edward 364
  John 577
  William B. 519
GILLESPIE, James 470
GILLIKIN, George A. 591
GLASGOW, James 503
GLAZIER, Ben. 635
GLOVER, John 168
  Jonathan 337
  William 21
GOELET, ___ 21
  Eliza 470
  John 21, 222, 364, 426, 500
GONDY, ___ 202
GOODE, Samuel 296
GOODMAN, William 479
GOODRICH, ___ 262
  Charles 140
GOODWIN, J. 291

GOODWIN (Cont.)
  Jonathan 222, 364
  William 12
GOOLD, Joseph 364
GOOSELY, George 6
  John 6
GORDON, B. 9
  George 470
  James 640
  Thomas 340, 500
GORE, Christopher 96
GORHAM, Ebenezer 390
  Hezekiah 591
GOUVERNEUR, Isaac 346
GRAHAM, Chas. 21
  Ebenezer 500
  Edward 446
  John 577
  Richard 411
GRANADE, Martin 591
GRANBERY, J. 555
  James 134, 305
  Josiah 222, 364, 602, 629
GRANDY, William 614
GRAY, Cornelius 91
  Stevens 108
  William Lee 108
GREEN, James 619
  Thomas K. 510
GREENLEAF, ____ 370
GREGORY, James 470, 591, 605
  Noah 91
GREY, Charles 240
GRICE, Charles 152, 434
  Charles, and Co. 73
  Frederick 441
GRIFFIN, Archibald 446, 454
  C. 145
  Frazer 291
GRIFFITH, Samuel 500
GRIMES, Wm. 454
GRISWOLD, Roger 625
GROVE, William Barry 198
  Wm. Barry 178
GROVER, James S. 500
GUITHER, John 195, 454
GUNN, James 84, 100
GURGENUS, Willie 619
GUYTHER, John 222
H_WELL, Sterling 256
HABERSHAM, Joseph 508
HACKET, James 430
HAFFORD (or HASSARD), George M. 328
HALEY, Nathan 431

HALL, ____ 385
  Benjamin 291
  Charles 260, 429
  Clement 204
  Edw. 192
  Edward 106, 461
  John 312, 394, 575
  Tim 635
HALSES, James 32
HALSEY, John 291, 500
HAM, George 168
HAMILTON, John 39, 195, 225, 228, 242, 333, 384, 408, 466
HAMLIN, Wood J. 446
HAMMON, Mary 364
HAMMOND, Abijah 246
  Jane 487
HANCOCK, ____ 417
HANKINS, Thomas 123, 364, 500, 577, 603
HARDELL, Josiah 12
HARDISON, Benjamin 409
HARDY, ____ 8
  Francis 577
  Humphrey 21, 509
  Miles 21
  Myles 505
  Robert 165
HARFORD, Henry 21
HARGROVES, ____ 621
HARPER, Robert Goodhue 59
  Robert Goodlee 82
  Robert Goodloe 277
HARRAMOND, Henry 577
HARRIS, Britain 454
  Charles W. 71
  Edmund 138
  James 372
  Martha 632
  Robert 161
HARRISON, Richard 445
  Thomas 472
HARTSHORE, ROBINSON and 275
HARTSHORN, William 225
HARVEY, Charles 26, 195
  Gracy 577
  John 7, 132, 339, 579
  Joseph 195, 441, 454
  Mary 26
  Polly 134
  T. 621
  Tho's. 104
  Thomas 212, 225
  Thomas H. 614
HARWOOD, John 222, 233

HASSELL, James 138
  John 138
  Joseph 138
  Zebedee 138
HATCH, Edmund 515, 527, 619
  John 454
  Joseph 619
HATHAWAY, James 226, 255, 408, 509, 627
  James, Sr. 144
HATTERSLEY, J. 184
HAUGHTON, Cha's. 291
  David 426
  Richard 591
HAWKS, Francis 520
HAWLEY, Daniel 626
HAYES, Joshua 356
HAYWARD, Samuel 600
HAYWOOD, Adam 583
  John 278, 456
HAZARD, George 364
HEARD, James 288
HEASTER, ___ 102
HEISTER, Joseph 263
HENDERSON, John 222
  Thomas 572
HENRY, Patrick 241, 257, 265
HERDRICK, Jabez 179
HERRING, Elias Langford 102
  William 102
HILL and PONS 21, 168
HILL, Henry 195, 454
  John 21, 454, 577, 614
  Jordan 583
  Samuel 619
  Thomas 577, 614
  William H. 583
  Wm. 291
  Wm. H. 454
HILLIARD, Jeremiah 583
HINCHIZ, T. 500
HINDMAN, William 249
HINES, Thomas 583
HODGE, John 127
HOGG, James 444
HOGSFLESH, Wm. 552
HOLLAND, Sarah 500
HOLLOWELL, Joel 132
HOLMES, ___ 71, 444
  Jas. 426
  Richard 621
HONEYWOOD, John 246
HOPKINS, ___ 511
  Samuel 296
HOPKINSON, Joseph 541

HORNIBLOW, John 301, 522, 577, 614
HORT (?), William 429
HOSKINS, James 454
  Richard 302
HOULY, Richard 614
HOWARD, John Egor 319
  Thomas 435
HOWCOTT, Nathaniel 190
HOWELL, David 210
HOWETT, Richard 21, 195
  Rowan 212
HOWITT, Sylvanus 104
HUBBARD, David G. 275
HUBBELL, Anson 168
  Walter 21, 222
  Walter, and Co. 259, 318
HUFFINS, ___ 345
HUGHES, Thos. H. 552
HULEN, Elias 577
HULL, James 224
HUMPHREY, Jas. 168
HUMPHREYS, ___ 43
  David 90, 133
  John 583
  Joshua 383
HUMPHRIES, John 97, 193
HUNLEY, Catharine 290
  Richard 290
HUNNINGS, Philip 138
HUNT, ___ 170
  Charles 222, 291
  John 417
HUNTER, ___ 629
  Archibald 446, 454
  Elisha 514
  Lewis 364
  Thomas 514, 534
  Timothy 21, 500
  W. 30
  William 168
HUSLRY (?), Josiah 168
HUTCHINGS, ___ 454
HYLTON and Co. 86
HYMAN, John 195, 454
IMIS (?), ___ 168
INDIANS
  Hanging Maw 115
  Scodacutta 115
INDIGO, John 635
INGLEE, Moses 542
INNES, James 96
IREDELL, James 86, 145, 265, 373
  Thomas 564
IRELAND, ___ 631

IRVINE, William 263
IRWIN, Jared 69
ISLAR, John 619
JACKSON, Bailey 441
  Baily 195
  Thomas 104
  Wm. 452
JACOCKS, Jonathan 104, 537
JAMES, Darkess 614
JAMISON, Ed. 552
JANSEN, C. W. 286
JANSON, C. W. 251, 291, 381, 565
  Charles W. 499
JARMAN, Hall 619
JARVIS, John 240
  Josiah 417
JAUNDUS, C. 591
JAY, ___ 285
  John 59
JEALLEN, John 577
JEFFERSON, ___ 228, 265
  Thomas 215, 270, 310, 319, 330
JEFFRY, ___ 345
JESSUP, William 319
JETT, Archibald 222
JOHERE, ___ 470
JOHNSON, Amos 454, 583
  Benoice 222
  Charles 629
  Holland 583
  John 168, 195
  Oliver 510
  Thomas 189, 441
JOHNSTON, Holland 454
  Jacob 619
  John 467
  Samuel 583
JONES, ___ 86, 511
  Allen 225
  Anne 455
  Arthur 614
  B. 103
  Benjamin 518
  David 394
  E. 291
  Elisha 426
  James 403, 417, 436, 454, 502, 583, 591
  Jemmy 530
  John 489
  John Paul 158
  Joseph 434
  Margaret 436, 502

JONES (Cont.)
  Marmaduke 291
  Mary 55
  Myles 91
  Peggy 434
  Richard 619
  Samuel, Jr. 529
  STEWART and 275
  Thomas 394, 455, 575
  William 12
  Willie 296, 444
JORDAN, Elizabeth 21, 76, 168
  J. 589
  Jacob 76
  James B. 21, 168, 441
  James Bruver 144
  Josiah 614
  Thomas 34, 104, 169
JOSELIN, Russell 614
JOURDAN, Elizabeth 217
JOUSH (?), John 161
JOYE, James 619
KEARNES, John 538
KEATON, Reuben 199, 200, 212, 273, 365, 366
KEENAN, T. 583
KEITH and TISDALE 491
KELLOG, Bradford 552
KELLY, George 42, 225, 280
  Patrick 291
  Shobel 291
KENNARD, Nathaniel 481
KENNEDY, Henry 291, 421
KENRICK, John 22
KERR, David 71, 577
  Edward 316, 353
KERWOOD, Nancy 104
KEYS, James 614
  James H. 291
  Jonathan 619
KIETH, BIXBY & 577
KIETH, Gabriel 161
KIMBERLY, Wm. 552
KIMBROUGH, Marmaduke 577
KING, Joseph 539
  Michael 393
  Rufus 133, 157
  Thomas 552
  William 620
KINSLEY, Apollus 295
KIP, ___ 253
KITTER, William 104, 222
KITTRELL, John 534
KNOX, Ambrose 75
  Andrew 75, 208

KNOX (Cont.)
  Henry 96
  Hugh 75, 208
KOCK, H. I. 21
KONIG, August 213
L'EVEILLE, ____ 327
LA FAYETTE, ____ 113
  George Washington Mot____ 113
LACOLESS, Michael 577
LACY, Joshua 394
LAILSON, ____ 584
LAMAR, Zaca. 139
LAMB, James 35
LAMBERT, Richard 511
LANCASHIER, John R. 104
LANCHESTER, Henry 159
LANDS, Seth 470
LANE, John 75, 155, 195, 422
LANG, ____ 335
  Betsey 426
LANGSTON, Demsey 58
LANKESTER, Henry 77
LARKINS, Jas. 583
LARUS, Philip 507
LATHARE, Daniel 470
LAUGHREA, Charles 12
LAUND, William M. 612
LAWLESS, Michael 612
LAWRENCE, Elisha 247
LAWRIE, William 142
LAWSON, Gavin 94
LEAVENS, Vine 614
LEE, B. 426
  Henry 145, 264, 364
  Thomas 187
LEECH, James 619
  Joseph 110, 394, 616
LEFFERTS, Leffert 335
LEICH, John 327
LEIGH, John 195, 290
LELVAUX, ____ 444
LEMMON, Richard 104, 222
LENOX, John 577
LEVY, Stephen 83
LEWIS, ____ 86
  John 417
  Josiah 583
  Mills 58
  Nicholas 196
  Ralph 91
  William 104, 364, 464
LIGHTBURN, Robert 406
  Samuel S. 406
LILLIBRIDGE, ____ 289
  Joseph 21, 426

LINDSAY, Adam 611
LISTE, Joseph 222
LITTLE, ____ 8
  F. 407
  John 8, 12, 342, 418
  William P. 583
LITTLEJOHN, Thomas B. 243, 300, 316
  Thomas B., and Co. 235, 292, 448, 496
  William 173, 236, 317, 550, 580
LIVERMORE, Edward St. Lue (?) 429
LIVINGSTON, Blockholst 530
  Edward 113
LOCKHART, ____ 136
LODGE, Giles 606
LONG, Azariah 21
  Benjamin 21, 542
  Isaac 104, 542
  James 138
  Joshua 21
  Nicholas 513
  Rebecca 291
  Rebeccah 168
  Thomas 168
LOOMIS and TILLINGHAST 275
LOOMISS, Nathaniel 454
LOPER, M. 621
LORILLARD, Peter 552
LOVE, James 291, 364
LOWTHER, HARDY and LITTLE 8
LOWTHER, Tristram 222
  William 118
LUMIN, John 635
LUSHLEY, Peter 396
LUTEN, King 523, 536
  Samuel 143
LUTON, King 168
LYON, Matthew 587
M'ALLISTER, Samuel 500
M'ALPINE, Niel 470
M'ARTHUR, Patrick 426
M'CANNA, Solomon James 426
M'CLELLAN, Malcolm 104
M'CLURE, Hugh 552
  Wm. 446
M'CLURG, James 225
M'COLLOM, Malcom 21
M'COLM, Malcolm 364
M'CONNELL, ____ 635
M'CORKLE, Samuel 71
M'COULSKY, James 621
M'COY, Thomas 500

M'COY (Cont.)
  William 21
M'DONALD, Duncan 104, 364
M'DOWELL, Joseph 211
M'DUGALD, Archibald 577
M'FARLANE, John 359
M'GLAUHN, Elisha 143
M'GLAUHON, John 63
M'GLOCKLIN, Patsey 614
M'HENRY, James 50, 56, 551
M'INNISH, Donald 104
M'INTOSH, James 335
M'INTYRE, Donald 470
  Gilbert 426
M'IVER, John 577
M'KEAN, Thomas 248, 263
M'KEEL, Mary 279
  Michael 279
M'KENZIE, Alexander 621
  Duncan 614
  George 614
M'KINLEY, James 291
M'KINNIE, John 501
M'KINZIE, Wm. 454
M'KOY, Malachi 614
M'LACHLAN, John 500
M'LAINE, Bab. 415, 470
M'LEAN, ___ 335, 583
M'LELLAN, Malcom 21
M'LEOD, Archibald 470
M'MILLAN, Daughald 500
M'MORINE, Robert 77, 501
M'NAIRY, John 114
M'NEEL, Archibald 577
  Niel 577
M'NIEL, Isabella 364
M'NULIE, James 614
MACARTHY, Daniel Bull 475
MACAULEY, Alexander 225
MACKAY, John 35
MACKENZY, George 550, 581
MACKEY, Huldah 40
  William 40
MACLAY, William 263
MACON, Nathaniel 211
MADISON, James 352
MADREN, Thomas 155
MAGEE, Ebenezer 614
MAIR, Samuel 426
MALEY, William 222
MALTBEE, Jonathan 51
MANDEVILLE, Mary 21
MANING, Edward 104
MANN, John 222, 233
MANNING, Benjamin 451

MANNING (Cont.)
  Edw'd. 222
  Edward 168
MARK, Solomon 619
MARKLAND, John 619
MARQUAND & STURGES 577
MARQUAND, Isaac 51
MARQUAND, PENFIELD and 99
MARRINER, ___ 36
MARRIOT, James 240
MARSH, Cyrus 52, 88
MARSHAL, John 395
MARSHALL, ___ 86
  Humphrey 62
  John 528
  Starling 317
  William 168
MARSTERS, Adam 635
MARSTON, John 275
MARTH, Saros 168
MARTIN, ___ 110
  Ambrose 321
  J. G. 280, 598
  Robert 104, 168
MASON, Abraham 21
MAT__ES, William 249
MATTHEWS, M. 296
MAXTON, Peter 450
MAYO, Nathan 195, 454, 583
MEREDITH, Samuel 23
  Sarah 476
MERRITT, Hezekiah 619
MESTA, Samuel 83
MICHAUX, X. 119
MIDER (?), Mason 12
MIELES, Hushin 470
MIFFLIN, ___ 285
MILBURN, Harry Clay 176
MILBURNE, Harry Clay 141
MILES, ___ 263
MILLEN, Alex'r. 305
  Alexander 29, 204
MILLER, ___ 317
  Edward 252
  Jas. 635
  Johannes 246
  Mary C. 104
MILLS, Benjamin 583
MING, Delilah 397
  Thomas 397
MITCHEL, L. S. 252
MITCHELL, Alexander 487
  John 485
MITHOLAND, Hugh 500
MIXON, Jeremiah 168

MOFFET, James 614
MOIGNARD, John Lewis Baptist 414
MONROE, ____ 201
MONTGOMERY (?), John 223
  Robert 223
MONTGOMERY, Robert 4, 195, 440, 454, 583
MOODY and AVERY 380, 526
MOODY, ____ 251
  Robert 93, 350, 419, 449
MOONEY, Lawrence 80
MOORE, A. D. 583
  Charles 192, 426
  Duncan 454
  Edward 358
  James 156, 500, 614
  Roger 467, 503
MORGAIN, William 619
MORGAN, ____ 263
  Daniel 319
  George 57
  Joseph 195
MORRIS, Aaron 291
  Aaron, Sr. 361
  Joseph 21
  Lewis 246
  Peter 473
  Robert 371, 409, 585
  Thomas 323
MORRISON, Michael 473
MORTON, George C. 626
  Hosea 417
MUNDEN, Levi 283
MURFREE, H. 135
  Hardy 204, 225
MURRAY, John 275
  Peter 468
MUSE, William T. 212, 344, 465
NANCE, Wynne 621
NARCROS, Nathaniel 345
  Samuel 345
NASH, Frederic 364
NEALE, Ab. 520
  Philip 583
NEEL, Sarah 614
NEGROES
  Abel (Abram) 348
  Abram 218
  Antomis 125
  Dick Pepper 550
  Dun 218
  Frank 451, 593
  George 98
  Harry 190, 376, 452

NEGROES (Cont.)
  Huse 638
  Isaac 493
  Israel 439
  Jacob Dun 576
  Jim 367
  Job 267
  Job (David Dave) 539
  John 125, 274
  Jude 64
  Murry 540
  Peter 64
  Prudence 196
  Rhody 439
  Robbin 594
  Simon 356
  Sip 581
  Tom 580
  York 586
NEIL, James 205
NEILSON, William 346
NELSON, John 247
  Thomas 120
NEVARRE, Bostin 337
NEW, Anthony 352
NEWBOLD, Caleb 247
NEWBY, Axum 222
  Exum 21, 291, 364, 577
  Francis 441
NEWKIRK, Charles 246
NEWMAN, Timothy 469
NEWSOME, James 143
NEWTON, Thomas 538, 598
NEXEN, E. 101
NICHOLLS, John 144, 168, 470
NICHOLS, Jehu 591
NICHOLSON, John 559
NICKERSON, Nathaniel 426, 614
NIEL, Honorie 402, 471
  James 21
NIELL, H. 45
NIHELL, Valentine 417
NIXON, ____ 620
  John 266
NORCOM, Frederick 18, 144, 271
  John 14, 426
  John, Jr. 364
  Joseph 271, 303
NORFLEET, B. 371, 640
  Benjamin 27
  E. 371, 640
  Elisha 27, 419, 493, 500
NORMAN, Henry 614
NORMON, Simeon 542
NOUGIER, Peter 438

NUTTING, Ebenezer 604
O'BRIEN, ___ 60, 224
  James 349
  Richard 43, 429
O'MALLEY, ___ 359, 407
  Matthew 316, 353
  Myles 107, 176, 316, 353, 364,
    568, 614
O'NEAL, Peter 364
OGDEN, Aron 247
  Lewis 284
OLIVER, Alexander 222
OSBORNE, Adlai 444
OSGOOD, Timothy 222
OTIS, John 291
  Joseph 419
  Nath. W. 419
OUTERBRIDGE, Stephen 222
OUTLAW, George 195, 441
OVERMAN, Thomas, Sr. 556
OWEN, William 631
PAINE, Ebenezer 586
  Nathaniel 103
  Thomas 24, 398
PALE, Christopher 614
PALIN, Lemuel 208
PALMER, William 394
PARKER, Benj. 83
  E. 621
PARKER (?), James 400
  John 58
  Robert 58
  Thomas 417, 575
PARMERLE, Benjamin 348
PARSONS, Charles 577, 591
  James 577, 591
PATTEN, Hans 441
PATTERSON, William 86
PATTERSONS, ___ 363
PATTON, Robert 323
PAYNE, Michael 151, 185, 202,
  274, 293, 316, 353, 518, 637
  Nathaniel 518
  Robert 296
PAYNTER, Susannah 591
PEACOCK, Samuel 577
PEALE, C. W. 227
PEARSON, Thomas 122
PEIRCE, Ezra 510
PENDER, Solomon 364, 577
PENDLETON, Frederick 344
  Timothy 365
  Zachariah 557
PENFIELD and MARQUAND 99
PEPPER, Samuel 577

PERKINS, Elisha 426
  John D. 426
  Noah 365
PERRY, Abner 143
  John 468
PERYNAUT, Francis 104
PETERSON, Henry 195
PETTIGREW, Charles 20, 364, 426,
  500, 591
PEYRENNAUT, Francis 222
PEYRINNAUT, Francis 364
PHELPS, Henry 531
  Oliver 174
PHILIPS, ___ 441
PHILLIPS, ___ 359
  Frederick 454
  G. N. 307, 355
  Gabriel N. 234
PHILLYAW, Martin 619
PHOENIX, Daniel 512
PICKERING, T. 357
  Timothy 48, 528
PIERCE, Charles 614
  Daniel 577
PINCKNEY, ___ 228
  Charles 607
  Charles C. 528
  Charles Cotesworth 201, 395
  Chas. C. 265
  Thomas 270, 319
  Thos. 265
  William 96
PINDAR, Jethro 348
PIPER, John 263
PIQUETT, Joseph 417
PLEDGER, Joseph 138
PLUMMER, Wm. S. 440
POLK, Ezekiel 467
  William 191, 237
POLLOCK, George 262, 619
POLLOK, ___ 561
  Ann B. 470
  Cullen 564
  George 564
  Thomas 104, 564
PONS, HILL and 21, 168
POOL, Joshua 200
  Thomas 267
PORIE, Francis 381
PORTER, John 291
POSNER, ___ 311
POYNER, Benjamin 426
  Thomas 144
PRENTICE, ___ 21
PRESCOT, Z. Currey 426

PRESSEY, Joseph 485
PRICE, David 577
  Jonathan 47
  William 575
  Wm. 417
PRIDE, Herbert 426
PRITCHARD, John 558
  Sarah 558
PUGH, Eaton 195
  Francis 98, 104, 168, 441
PURDIE, Ivey 577
PURDY, Ivey 482
PURVIANCE, S. 583
QUIGLEY, Cornelius S. 364
RABEL, Jean 379
RACHEL, ____ 566
RAMCKE, ____ 258, 516
  Frederick 165, 364, 614
RAMSAY, Allen 272, 340
RANDALL, Robert 33
RANDOLPH, Charles 614
RASOR, Josiah 414
RAVENS, John 426
RAY, Daniel 577
READING, Joseph 360
REDDICK, James 132
REDDITT, Josiah 351
REDMAN, John 453
REED, Christian 364
  Christopher 291
  Nicholas 577, 591, 614
RELFE, Enoch 447, 465
RELLY, Patrick 222
REYNOLDS, John 6
  William 6
RHEA, Jonathan 247
RHODES, J. T. 583
  Thomas 614
RICE, Benjamin 364
  David 21
RICHARDS, ____ 444
  Elizabeth 621
RICHARDSON, Joseph 378
RIDDICK, David 364
  Jos. 514
  Joseph 195, 454, 464
  Micajah 58
  Robert 591
  Solomon 132
RIEVES, John 53
RIGHT, ____ 621
RILEY, Edward 364
RIPLEY, Spencer 28
RIPLY, ____ 501
RITTENHOUSE, David 310

ROANE, Archibald 114
ROBERTS, ____ 345
  Charles 196
  Sarah 592
  William 129
  Willis 592
ROBERTSON, Will. 84
ROBINSON and HARTSHORE 275
ROBUCK, John 104
RODDY, Josiah 591
RODMAN, Gilbert 168
RODNEY, E. 500
  Henry 364
ROEBUCK, John 168
ROGERS, John 583
  Jonathan 58
  Thomas 417
ROGGERSON, Isaiah 132
ROMAYNE, N. 445
RONDET, ____ 176, 426
RONOK, Goston 222
ROOT, William 246
ROSE, Peyton 426
ROSS, John 500
  Martin 104, 426
  Mary 364
  Peter 591
ROWAN, Archibald Hamilton 486
  John 306
  Robert 104, 222
RUMBOUGH, Wm. 291
RUSSEL, ____ 345
  John 420
RUSSELL, Edward 291
  Timothy 289
RUTHERFORD, John 247
RUTLEDGE, Edward 607
  John, Jr. 277
  William 375
RYAN, George 104
  Thomas 426
SACKVILLE, ____ 506
SAMS, Edmund 161
SANDERLIN, Devotion 91
SANSBURY, Hillery 576
SARGENT, Winthrop 541
SATTERFIELD, Thomas 88, 580
SAUL, John 619
SAUNDERS, James 222, 364
SAWYER, ____ 624
  Asa 91
  David 426
  Enoch 426
  Evan 91
  Frederick B. 212

SAWYER (Cont.)
  Lemuel 91
  Malachi 91, 364, 426
  Willis 91, 517
SCARBOROUGH, Benjamin 104
  William 104
SCOTT, John B. 296
  Lydia 614
SCULL, John G. 621
SEABOURN, Isaac 222
SEAGROVE, James 139
SEAMAN, Thomas 10, 286, 326, 347, 639
SEGEAUD, John B. 154
SEIVER, John 114
SESSIONS, ____ 621
SESSUMS, George W. 143
SEWAIN, Jeremiah 138
SEYMOUR, ____ 470
SHANNONHOUSE, James L. 77
SHARROCK, Thomas 364
SHAW, John 212, 387
SHEEL, Martin 172, 213, 219, 258, 291
SHEPHERD, Joseph 500
SHERWOOD, Nancy 21
SHINE, Daniel 619
  John 619
SHINGSTON, Sarah 500
SHIPPER, ____ 620
SHIRTLISS (or SHIRTLIFF), ____ 518
SHREEVE, John 377
SIBBALD, Fanny 285
  George 36
SIGAUD, ____ 381
SILBY, Henry 454
SILLIMAN, Isaac 291
SILVESTER, Mary 417
SIMMONS, James m. 84
  Jesse 195, 428
SIMMS, James 84
SIMONS, Charlton 14
  Jacob 220
  John 220
SIMPSON, Evan 168
  James 38, 66
  John 364, 621
  Samuel 454
SINCLAIR, George 83
SINGLETON, Spyers 572
SKINNER, Evan 222
  John 441, 572
  Joshua 21, 434
  Nathan 376

SKINNER (Cont.)
  William 7, 504, 579
SLABURY, Samuel 85
SLADE, Ebenezer 195
  Jeremiah 454, 583
  William 608
SLAUGHTER, A. 280
  Augustine 538, 598
SMALL, John 21
SMITH, ____ 105, 253, 417, 583
  Abraham (?) 263
  Albert 582
  Benjamin 296
  Eliza 364
  Elizabeth 291
  Emos 426
  Granville 364
  James 532
  Jeremiah 429
  John 394, 575
  Joseph 577
  Michael 37
  N. 583
  Naire 411
  Oliver 125, 591
  Pardon 411
  Peter 246
  Robert 104, 207, 426
  S. 95
  Samuel 33, 249, 566
  T. 325
  Thomas 58
  W. 304
  William 33, 277, 417, 426, 429
  William T. 492
  Wm. 635
SMITHSON, Albert 161
SNOW, R. 253
SNOWDEN, Nathan 195
SOWELL, James 143
SPAIGHT, R. D. 256
  Richard Dobbs 571, 583
SPARK, Thomas 591
SPARKES, Thomas 577
SPEIGHT, Francis 479
SPENCE, John 91
SPENCER, Zachariah 575
SPEREMENTS, F. 104, 222
SPERIMENTS, F. 364
SPILLER, Henry 593
  Wm. 500
SPOONER, Charles 577
SPRIGG, Richard 249
SPRING, Samuel 411

SPRUIL, Charles 542
  Demsey 542
SPRUILL, Benjamin 426
  Charles 195, 454
  Chas. 21
  Samuel 138
  William 138
SPURR, Benjamin 439
SQUIRES, R. A. 443, 567
ST. BARBE, Wyatt 170
STAFFORD, Stephen 591, 614
  Thomas 132
STALLINGE, Jesse 144
STALLINGS, Luke 132
  Nicholas 76
  S. 583
STALLION, Luke 353
STANDIN, H. 27
  Hend. 21, 168, 291, 364, 426, 500, 591
  Henderson 239, 470, 522, 573, 577, 614
  Lemuel 104, 222
STANDLEY, Evan 91
STANDLY, David 593
STANLEY, John 583
STANSBURY, Joseph 512
STEEL, John 541
STEELE, Elizabeth 426
  John 171
STEPHENS, John 240
  Thomas 240
STEPHENSON, Luther 104
STEPNEY, William 144
STETSON, Theophilus 426
STEVENSON, Henry 319
STEWART and JONES 275
STEWART, David 95
  John 195
STITSON, Wm. 591
STODDARD, Samuel 222
STODDER, Ben. 615
  Benjamin 543
STONE, B. 489
  David 11, 168, 334, 548
  Hezekiah 168
  Zedekiah 225, 334
STONS, Roger 364
STORY, Wm. W. 512
STOTT, Ebenezer 184
  Watson 184
STRAN, ____ 83
STREET, Samuel 364
STRONG, John 21
STUART (?), James 114
STUART and BARR 387
STUART, John 614
STUBBS, Abner 222
  William 138, 560
STURGES, Balow 21
STURGES, MARQUAND and 577
STURGES, Thomas 542
SULLIVAN, James 210
SUMLER (?), Thomas 277
SUMNER, Polly 434
SUMPTER, ____ 351
SUTTON, James 186
  Lemuel 21, 168, 614
  Wm. 291, 500
SWAN, R. 500
SWANN, Rebecca 470
SWEPSON, Thomas 225
SYLVESTER, Elizabeth 575
SYMONS, John 266
TABB, J. A. 195
  James 446
TAGERT, John 614
TAGGART, Joseph 46
TAIT, William 614
TATOM, Absalom 572
TAYLOR, Allen 437
  Benjamin 426
  Geo., Jr. 81
  James 619
  John 275, 591
TAZEWELL, Henry 630
TEMPLE, John 370
TEN BROECK, Abraham 246
THATCH, Leaven 132
THATCHER, ____ 412
THOMAS, ____ 577, 591, 614
  Nancy 577
THOMPSON, Henry D. 168
  J. 583
  Raphael 575
  Thomas 430
  Thomas Wm. 268
  William 49, 577
  Wm., Jr. 591
THOMSON, Sarah E. 546
  William 426
  Wm. 524
  Wm., Jr. 497
THORN, Martha 168
THORNDIKE, Israel 240
THORNE, Richard 246
THORNTON, Thomas 619
THURLO, ____ 210
TILGHMAN, ____ 33
  Edward 86

TILLINGHAST, LOOMIS and 275
TILLMAN, Henry 446
TILTON, Daniel 541
TISDALE, KEITH and 491
TODDNY, ____ 417
TOLER, James 554
TOMLINSON, Isaac 214
TORKSEY, ____ 441
TOWERS, John 459
TRACY, James 83
TREADWAY, William 161
TREADWELL, Chas. 622
TREDWELL, Samuel 182
TROTTER, Thomas 364, 426
TRUEBLOOD, John 299
   Timothy 306
TRUMBULL, John 269
TRUXTON, Thomas 544
TUCK, John 500
TUCKER, Tudor 485
TURNER, James 29, 351, 583
   John 169
   Kinchen 426
TUYLER, William 577
TWINE, Abraham 132
   Jesse 132
TYLER, ____ 345
   Samuel 405
   William 345
   Wm. 591
TYRREL, Wm. 503
UDALL, Daniel 291
ULVIER, Joshua 614
UNDERWOOD, John 485
USHER, ____ 94
VAIL, John 144, 162, 354, 540, 614
   Thomas 426, 614
VALENTINE, Elizabeth 255
VAN RENSELLAER, ____ 368
VAN RENSSELAER, Robert 246
VAN VECHTEN, Abraham 246
VERELL, John 405
VERREE, Joseph 159
VEVIER, ____ 591
VOLFER (or VOLSER), P. 104
VREDENBURG, ____ 101
WAGNER, Jacob 338, 570
WAGSTAFF, David 275
WALKER, Edward 138
   Henry 294
   James 583
   Thomas 291
WALKERS, Thomas 364
WALLACE, John 104, 291

WALLASTON, Frederick H. 429
WALMSBRY, John 591
WALMSLEY, John 577
WALTON, ____ 629
   John B. 195
   Timothy 195, 500
WARBRITTON, William 2
WARBUTTON, William 577
WARD, Francis 417
   George 619
   James 577
   James T. 516
   John 583
   Michael 577, 591, 614
WARE, ____ 86
WARNIER, Angel 591
WARREN, Henry 419
WARREN (?), I. 248
WARRENTON, Thomas 470
WARRICK, Henry 426, 471
WARRING, Hambleton 1105, 291
   John 222
WASHINGTON, ____ 265
   Bushrod 590
   G. 269
   George 48, 270, 319, 562
   William 319
WATERMAN, Stephen 591
WATERS, Isaac 202
WATSON, J. 454
   John 552
WAYNE, Anthony 166, 297, 319
WEADON, John 364
WEAKLY, ____ 621
WEATHERSPOON, Daniel 619
WEBB, BRYER and Co. 222
WEBB, John, Jr. 161
   Zachariah 439
WEEKS, Reuben 552
WELLS, ____ 566
   Gurden 104, 222
   Samuel 291
WELROY, William 74
WENTWORTH, Tilley 577, 591
WEST, Betsey 168
   Geo. 21, 577
   George 564
   Henry 161
   Joshua 591
WESTBROOK, James 619
WHEATON, Daniel 620
   William 426
   Wm. 579
WHEDBEE, Samuel 366
   Thomas 303

WHEDBEE (Cont.) 64
WHEELER, John 259
  Solomon 614
WHITALL, Zatthu M. 426
WHITE, ___ 168, 621
  Charles 399
  John 614
  John D. 542
  Joseph 441
  Joseph, Jr. 313
  Joshua 12
  Simson 614
  Thomas 364, 368, 426, 470, 500
WHITEHILL, John 263
WHITEMORE, Ephraim 364
WHITFIELD, Lewis 168
WHITING, Abner 470
  Samuel 104, 291, 470, 500
WHITMORE, Ephraim 591
  Nathaniel 437
WICHELHAUSEN, Frederick Jacob 147
WICKS, James 619
WIGGENS, Blake B. 614
WIGGINS, ___ 500, 635
  Thos. 583
WILBY, Hillery 58
WILCOCKS, ___ 86
WILDER, Willis 12
WILKINS, ___ 253
WILKINSON, George 601
  William D. 614
WILLCOCKS, Wm. 112
WILLIAMS, Ann 603
  Arthur 367
  Asa 365
  Benj. 444
  Benjamin 98
  Christopher 635
  Elisha 426
  Elizabeth 123, 222
  Isaac 468
  J. B. 494
  James 364
  Jesse 358
  John 222, 444, 549
  Joseph J. 572
  Robert, Jr. 203, 427, 460
  Samuel 369
  Thomas 138, 195, 426
  Thomas P. 230
  Willis 123
  Wm. 522, 591
WILLIAMSON, Benjamin 195, 446

WILLIS, ___ 468
  John 21, 168
  William 429
WILLOCK, Thomas 280
WILLS, ___ 111, 138, 461
  H. 483
  Henry 151, 238, 442, 522, 573, 574, 610, 618
  James 483, 484
WILSON, ___ 474
  Ben. 488
  Daniel 405
  George, Sr. 362
  James 86, 590
  John, Sr. 296
  Lem. 144
  Malachi 21
  Michael 104, 222
  Stephen 91
  Willis 417
WINCHESTER, James 114
WINDSHIP, Amos 364
WINSLOW, Joshua 178
WINTER, James 291
WINTHROP, John 345
WIRE, Joshua 577
WITHERINGTON, Charlton 144
WOLSEY, Malachi 470
WOOD, ___ 265
  James 274, 303
  John 21
  Jus. 492
WOODARD, John 104
WOODBURY, Joshua 531
WOODLEY (?), Hezekiah 199
WOODLEY, Willis 341
WOODWARD, James 12
  John 168, 222
WORLEY, Thomas 393
WRIGHT, ___ 629
  William E. 422
WYATT, John 21
  Sackar 138
WYLLYS, George 121
WYNKOOP, Benjamin 156, 252
WYNN, Wm. 566
WYNNE, George 138
WYNNES, Penelope 364
WYNNS and BRICKELL 614
WYNNS and BRICKLE 364
WYNNS, Thomas 80, 195, 583
  Thos. 454
  W. 143
  William Baker 80
YANCEY, Sterling 583

YATES, Abraham, Jr. 181
   John 621
YOUNG, Daniel 457
   John 143, 222, 403
   Nicholas 126
YOUNG, MILLER and Co. 317
YUNDT, ____ 459
YZNARDI, Joseph M. 66

www.ingramcontent.com/pod-product-compliance
Lightning Source LLC
Chambersburg PA
CBHW042358070526
44585CB00029B/2984